Dix Bruce's
Gypsy Swing
& Hot Club Rhythm

Complete
Mandolin Edition

- Gypsy Swing Vol. 1 & Vol. 2 books combined into one volume

- 5 new songs!

- Learn melodies & chord progressions to 29 great Gypsy Swing songs in the style of Django Reinhardt, Stephane Grappelli, and the Quintette of the Hot Club of France

- Learn moveable closed-position swing/jazz chords

- Learn the swing mandolin rhythm "comp"

- Download and jam along with a great Hot Club-style band

- Play along and practice rhythm and soloing. *We'll jam all night long!*

- Music includes standard notation, mandolin tablature, chords, lyrics

- Bonus downloadable music and exercises!

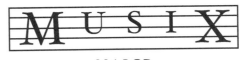

906 BCD

Cover design by Charlotte Gibb. Back cover photo of Dix Bruce by Theresa Hioki.
Thanks to Brian Lambert, Sherry Shachter, Bruce Pettit, Marjorie McWee, Gayle Forner, Brandt Williams, and Kathi Bruce for their most helpful suggestions. Book and recordings © Copyright 2007, 2008, 2020 by Dix Bruce.
Musix, P.O. Box 30936, Walnut Creek, CA 94598 • www.musixnow.com

11-1-20

Contents

Introduction

In 2007 I went to a weekend-long Django Reinhardt festival south of San Francisco. The performers were some of the leading players of Gypsy Swing/Jazz from around the world. The music was fantastic – beautifully played and wonderfully exciting.

But it was the unexpected scene around the theater that captured my attention. Everywhere, down the block, in front of the theater, in the lobby, hallways and staircases, were knots of two and three musicians jamming their hearts out on standards from the Hot Club Swing repertoire. All around the venue musicians wore their guitars on their backs or held their violins in their hands ready to jam at any opportunity. Wherever there was an empty square yard of space, small groups of musicians assembled, played a bit, broke up, and reassembled to play more. I was amazed at the number of audience members who came to the festival ready to play and at their fervent efforts to connect with other like-minded musicians and jam on a few tunes in between the main acts on the stage. Something was definitely happening here. I'd had no idea that Gypsy Swing had become so popular.

But why not? Gypsy Swing, popularized initially in the mid-1930s by Django Reinhardt, Stephane Grappelli, and the Quintette of the Hot Club of France, is exceptional and exciting music. I discovered it myself in the 1970s and have worked on learning it for over forty years. Even after all that time I'm still awed by the original recordings of Django and Stephane and the Hot Club Quintette. I hear more in their music and learn from it each time I listen.

That original Gypsy Swing sound, especially the playing of Reinhardt and Grappelli, has inspired musicians for over eighty years. Based on American swing and jazz, played instrumentally on American pop songs of the early 20th century plus Django and Stephane's original compositions, the Quintette mixed in sounds from eastern and western Europe and from Django and Stephane's experiences and cultures. Django brought the Gypsy element, Stephane his French-Italian heritage and pan-European sensibilities.

Most unusually, the Quintette was a purely acoustic, all-strings band: Django on lead guitar, Stephane on violin, two rhythm guitarists, plus string bass. No horns, no drums, no electrics, even though those sounds were prominent in the dominant musical styles of the day. And the Quintette's music spoke boldly and swung mightily. When you listen to their recordings you won't believe their virtuosity, intensity, or the fire with which they played. Musicians, string players especially, hear that passion and energy and think, "I want to do *that*!"

Of course Gypsy Swing, like any other style of great music, is not easy to play. It requires a deep knowledge of early 20th century pop songs, chords, melodies, and an ability to physically play all three on an instrument. How does one get started when there's so much to know and such a steep learning curve? How can you play in a band until you've worked out these basics?

Seeing all those impassioned and aspiring Gypsy Swing musicians hungry to play with others got me thinking. I'd always found that the best, quickest, easiest, and most fun way to learn music was by playing with a band. I wondered if I could put together a book/audio combination with a recorded Gypsy Swing band that students could play along with, to learn chords, chord progressions, melodies, songs, and to practice soloing. It would have to be something dynamic that provided a way for musicians to work and practice the basics, at both slow and regular speeds, over and over again until chords, progressions, melodies, songs, and soloing became comfortable and second nature. That would be a great way to prepare musicians to jam with others or play in a band. **Gypsy Swing and Hot Club Rhythm** was the result.

The original 12-song **Gypsy Swing and Hot Club Rhythm** book and recording sets (one each for guitar and mandolin) were published in 2007. They were popular enough that I put together a second 12-song volume the following year entitled **Gypsy Swing and Hot Club Rhythm, Vol. II**, again one each for guitar and mandolin. In 2020 I decided to combine both of these volumes, plus a few additional tunes and recordings, into **Gypsy Swing and Hot Club Rhythm Complete** with separate mandolin and guitar editions.

My sincere hope is that the materials in this book will help you learn to play rhythm and leads, chords, melodies, chord progressions, and songs, and prepare you to jam with other Gypsy Swing musicians, maybe even form a band, and have a great time playing this magnificent music!

Dix Bruce – Fall 2020

Dix Bruce

*Dix Bruce is a writer and award-winning musician from the San Francisco Bay Area. He edited David Grisman's **Mandolin World News** from 1978 to 1984. He has produced over sixty instructional book/ audio sets and videos, most for Mel Bay Publications. His most recent videos are "Swing & Jazz Mandolin: Chords & Rhythm" and "Mandolin Licks-er-cises." Dix has played guitar with San Francisco's Royal Society Jazz Orchestra since the late 1980s. Visit him online at www.musixnow.*

Gypsy Swing and Hot Club Rhythm

The music of the **Quintette of the Hot Club of France** with **Django Reinhardt** on guitar and **Stephane Grappelli** on violin is a kind of mystic holy grail for fans of string swing and jazz. Django and Stephane played with exceptional virtuosity, passion, excitement, and a life force that's still infectious almost seventy years after they played their last notes together. The sound is, at times, unbelievable. How could human beings play with such precision and fire? And their music swings! When you hear it, you want to play along!

The purpose of this book and recording is to get you started playing music in the **Gypsy Swing and Hot Club** style on the mandolin. You'll first learn "swing" chords and Hot Club-style rhythm while playing 29 great songs along with the recorded Hot Club-style bands. After that you can concentrate on learning the melodies and practice playing leads. Finally, you'll develop your own solos and rehearse them with the band that never gets tired. In addition to having a lot of fun while improving your strength and stamina as a player, you'll build a repertoire of songs, chords, chord progressions, melodies, and leads.

Start by reading the music in the book and playing along with the recorded rhythm sections, first at a slow speed with just guitar accompaniment, then, when you're ready, with the full-blown Hot Club-style band. The band will play through each tune several times to give you the opportunity to practice rhythm chords, melodies, and your own solo improvisations. It's just like having your own band on call. You can work on chord changes, a tune, solo, or passage for hours, perfecting it without wearing out your fellow players. The opportunities for advancing your reading and improvising skills while expanding your repertoire are unlimited. *We'll jam all night long!*

Most of the songs and chord progressions in the book were recorded by Django Reinhardt and Stephane Grappelli and are important standards both in the Gypsy Swing world and in the larger worlds of Swing and Jazz. The music includes standard notation, tablature, chords, lyrics, chord diagrams, and suggested fingerings.

For the most part, the songs are presented in the keys the Hot Club played them in. There are exceptions, and I took some liberties here and there for the sake of variety and harmonic interest. One of my goals with this project is to help make keys interchangeable to you and prepare you to play *any song in any key* with ease. Learning closed-position chords and melodies will give you a great head start. Throughout the book I'll encourage you to move melodies and solos around the fingerboard. Use the *Scale, Chord, and Transposition Chart* on page 74 to help you understand chords in various keys and how to transpose. It shows all the major scales and chords for every key. It's a great tool for transposing.

Measure numbers are shown above the treble clef sign on the left side of each song beginning with the second staff. I refer to these numbers in the text accompanying the songs. Numbering starts after any pickup measures.

I added circles to the tablature numbers to represent half notes or longer so they more accurately reflect the standard notation. See the example at the top of page 7.

Melodies and rhythm section back ups to all the tunes in this book are recorded at slow and regular speeds. First you'll hear a melody played on mandolin slowly, with just guitar back up. Then you'll hear the same melody at regular speed, with the full band, including rhythm mandolin. Finally you'll hear the band playing the song from beginning to end, several times through, without any recorded lead. You'll play all the chords, melodies, solos and improvisations! Here's the link to download the recordings: **musixnow.com/gsaudiomando/** If you'd prefer to have the recordings on CD use this link to order: **musixnow.com/gypsy-swing-hot-club-rhythm-complete-mandolin-edition/**

Most melodies are written with all fretted notes. Some include open-string notes to make them easier to play. As soon as you learn a melody with open-string notes, change these to fretted notes so they'll be more easily moved around the fingerboard. All chords are shown in closed positions with no open strings. Beginning and intermediate mandolinists tend to perceive melodies or chords with open-string notes as somehow easier than those with all closed-position or fretted notes. That may be because melodies or chords with open-string notes are more familiar than those with all closed-position notes. However, there's a great advantage to knowing chords and melodies in closed positions.

Closed-position chords and entire chord progressions as well as closed-position melodies and solos can be easily moved up and down the fingerboard to new positions and keys. Why would we want to move a song to a different key? Suppose you learn "Avalon" as written in the key of F. Great, as long as the people you play with perform it in the same key. You might come across a tenor sax player who wants to play the song in the key of Ab. Or, perhaps, a singer might need to sing "Avalon" in the key of Bb. If you know the chord progression or melody in a closed position, you simply move everything, chords, melodies, improvisations, up or down the fingerboard to the new key.

The small numbers between the lyric and tablature lines are suggested fretting finger numbers for melodies. If you can't reach the notes with the suggested fingers, feel free to change them. Chord diagrams include the same information and are explained further in the "Swing Mandolin Rhythm" section on page 11.

The first twelve songs in the book, pages 13 through 45, are from the original **Gypsy Swing and Hot Club Rhythm** book. The recorded back up bands for these songs play in the style of the Quintette of the Hot Club of France. Band #1 includes Jason Vanderford on rhythm guitar, Steve Hanson on string bass, and me, Dix Bruce, on rhythm guitar and mandolin. I also play the mandolin leads.

Songs thirteen through twenty-four, pages 46 through 87, are from my second publication, **Gypsy Swing and Hot Club Rhythm, Vol. II**, played by Band #2: Jason Vanderford on rhythm guitar, Marty Eggers on string bass, and me on rhythm guitar, mandolin, and mandolin leads.

The remaining 5 songs were recorded during both sessions and are published here for the first time. The band for each song is identified in the song introduction.

The Bands

Photo by Kathi Bruce

L. to R.: Jason Vanderford, Steve Hanson, Dix Bruce, Band #1.

Photo by Theresa Hioki

L. to R.: Jason Vanderford, Marty Eggers, Dix Bruce, Band #2.

How to Work with the Book and Recordings

• **Download the play-along audio for this book: musixnow.com/gsaudiomando/** Each song in **Gypsy Swing & Hot Club Rhythm Complete** has three accompanying audio tracks: the mandolin melody played slow with just guitar accompaniment, the mandolin melody played up-to-speed with the band, and the play-along band track where you supply all the rhythm chords and leads. Each file is named accordingly. For example the three "Avalon" tracks are named like this: "Avalon slow M.mp3" "Avalon up-to-speed M.mp3," "Avalon track M.mp3." Some songs have additional bonus tracks.

• **Before you dive into a chord progression or melody, read along with the music as you first listen to the recording.** It's a good idea to review the chords and scales of the key each song is in, especially if you are not used to playing in that key. Learn the chords and chord progressions by playing along with the slow version first. Gradually work your way up to the up-to speed band version. If you're new to this style of music, there will be a lot to learn: chords in different positions, the rhythm comp, and the melody — not to mention any solos you develop or improvise.

• **If the recordings are too fast for you to play along with,** use software like "The Amazing Slow Downer" to slow them down. "Audacity" software can also be used to slow audio down. Try practicing each song with a metronome at slower tempos. Online metronomes and downloadable apps are readily available. Learning to play along with a metronome is a valuable skill for any musician. Sight read through a piece a few times, then set the metronome to a speed slow enough to play it top to bottom without stopping and restarting. This slow speed should be set at a tempo where you can successfully play the most difficult passage of a song. As you work on a song gradually increase the metronome speed.

• **After you've memorized the chords and the chord progression, try playing the melody along with the recording,** again mastering the slow version before you move on to the full-speed band version. Memorize the melody. This will make soloing, whether stating some version of the melody or improvising, much easier. Then try moving the melody up or down an octave, whatever the instrument allows. If the melody includes open-string notes, find their fretted equivalents and transpose these melodies too.

• **Once you can play the melody along with the band, try making up your own solos.** Start by changing the memorized melodies slightly as you play along to make them swing more than the versions on the printed page. By "rhythmizing" a melody you can create an entirely new solo. I demonstrate this technique on several of the songs including "After You've Gone" on page 18 and "Chicago" on page 25. As mentioned above, try transposing the melody up or down an octave from where it's written. We'll work through that on "The Sheik of Araby" on page 32. Work through these exercises again and again until you have something that feels like your own solo. Remember, the recorded band will back you up for hours with no complaints as you try this melody or that lick.

• **It's always a good idea to write out your improvisations and keep them in a spiral bound music notebook.** That way you can refer back and revise them as you progress. Work with the slow recording of a song until you're ready for the full-speed band version. You can isolate the lead or rhythm part from either version by simply adjusting the balance control on your player. If you're listening with headphones or earbuds you can take one side off. "Audacity," mentioned above as a "slo-downer," allows you to import audio and control the pan of the playback through your computer or smart phone.

• **Listen to how mandolinists and other musicians that you admire play these songs and how they solo on them.** The most obvious place to start is with the masters: Django Reinhardt and Stephane Grappelli. Listen closely and try to analyze how they approach a melody or chord progression. Be encouraged to "borrow" from Django, Stephane, or other masters. Learn their vocabularies and how they assemble phrases into a coherent whole. Learning to improvise in music is a lot like learning to speak. We all have the same letters, words and phrases which we continually recycle into sentences and paragraphs that, hopefully, express what we're feeling. Same with music: the goal is to build your own musical vocabulary which will allow you to speak through your instrument. There are countless reissues of the music of the Quintette of the Hot Club of France and of Django and Stephane's recordings. Some of the best and most economical are the four and five disc sets on JSP Records. I recommend "Django Reinhardt: The Classic Early Recordings in Chronological Order" (JSPCD901), "Django Reinhardt Vol. 2: Paris and London 1937 to 1948" (JSPCD904), and "Django in Rome 1949/1950" (JSP919). Stephane Grappelli is included in all three sets. The first consists mainly of classic Hot Club material, and in order to understand the music in this book, you really must hear it. "Django in Rome 1949/1950" is superb and interesting in that it presents Django and Stephane with a more "modern," non-Hot Club style rhythm section with piano, bass, and drums. All of it is great music!

• **As you're listening for inspiration, don't limit yourself to mandolinists.** Listen to everybody that you think is great, no matter what instrument they play. Identify what it is about a musician's playing or singing that moves you. Try to incorporate some of that into your own playing. Make yourself curious enough to listen to your favorite recorded musicians play a lick or passage until you figure it out — a hundred times if necessary. Violin and mandolin share the same tuning. Can you adapt something Stephane Grappelli plays to the mandolin?

• **Experiment with leaving the melodies completely behind.** Sing along with the tracks and vocalize your ideas. Learn to sing what you're trying to play, even if you think you have a lousy voice. Look for new ideas and input constantly, and try to make them a part of your playing. Practice playing whatever is in your mind and heart. Don't quit working with the track after one solo — especially if it doesn't sound as good as you want it to right away — work it through the whole track. One of the advantages of the back up track is that you can try out an idea and play it on several solos in succession. You'll gradually gain control of it as you repeat it.

• **Make the recorded band *your* band and work out with it daily.** The more you play, the better you'll play. You'll gain strength, stamina, and focus as you train yourself to play two, three, four or more solos in a row. A typical gig might consist of four forty-five minute sets with fifteen minute breaks in between. Start by jamming along with the band for ten to fifteen minutes a day and work up from there. If you play enough you'll eventually find that ideas and solos will begin to emerge and flow. It will be a great and rewarding process of discovery!

Check out my other "play along with the band" sets: **BackUP TRAX: Swing & Jazz** (includes mandolin TAB), **BackUP TRAX: Early Jazz & Hot Tunes**, and **BackUP TRAX: Traditional Jazz & Dixieland**. Though **Early Jazz** and **Traditional Jazz** don't include TAB, you'll still enjoy jamming along. Full details and samples are available on my web site: **musixnow.com**.

Author Michael Dregni wrote a very interesting biography of Django Reinhardt titled "Django: The Life and Times of a Gypsy Legend" (Oxford University Press). For more information on Stephane Grappelli, you'll love the 2-DVD release "A Life in the Jazz Century" (Music on Earth). It includes all known film footage of Django Reinhardt.

Swing Mandolin Rhythm

Swing mandolin rhythm is a combination of two elements:

- closed-position moveable chords, and
- the "comp" or pulse of those strummed closed-position chords.

In many styles of music, chords are strummed and the notes are allowed to ring. In swing and jazz we use closed-position chords with no open-string notes because we want to be able to control how long the notes of the chord ring to set up our rhythmic groove. We also want these chords to be moveable to other positions and keys.

The familiar G7 below left has open-string notes. If we strum the chord, strings three and four (string one is the thinnest on your mandolin and shown on the right in chord diagrams, string four the fattest and shown on the left in chord diagrams) will continue to ring even if we lift our first and second fingers after we strum the chord. The G7 on the right below is a closed-position form with no open-string notes. The "x" under string one of the chord diagram tells us to mute or not play that string. (The open first string E note is not part of the G7 chord.) In this closed G7 form the side of my first finger mutes the first string. The "r" under string four of the G7 at left shows where the root (G in this G7 chord) is located if it's present in the form. Many of the chord forms we'll use, like the G7 on the right, don't include a root. Muting the chord while strumming is accomplished by loosening the fretting hand grip just enough after the strum to stop the sound. The number to the right of some of the chord diagrams tells us at which fret to place the form. (See the first C7 chord on page 13.)

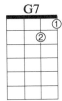

Chord diagrams are shown with the individual songs in the approximate order they appear in a progression. In some cases alternate fingerings or forms are also given. Try them all and see how each works in a particular situation. One might sound better or be easier to move in and out of than another. Try substituting different versions of the same chord from other songs in the book. Each form has a slightly different tonal color but an A7 is an A7 is an A7. For the sake of the rhythmic comp, we'll use closed chord forms with no open-string notes. Swap out chords of the same quality: an A7 for an A7, an Am6 for an Am6, but not an A7 for an Am6.

The "comp" is a pattern of strumming with the picking hand and pulsing with the fretting hand to set up a groove that propels the rhythm. Let's look at 4/4 rhythm, which is the most prevalent meter in Swing and Gypsy Swing. In 4/4 we play four beats to the measure: 1 – 2 – 3 – 4. To play the basic comp we let strums one and three ring a bit, but mute two and four right after they're played. That gives the kind of "cha – chuk – cha – chuk" rhythm that Django and Stephane usually had behind them in the Quintette. According to Michael Dregni, the author of "Django: The Life and Times of a Gypsy Legend," this rhythm became known as *la pompe* or "the pump." Dregni describes it as: "striking each beat with a percussive strum, any sustain choked off by dampening the strings immediately after the downward strum." Listen to the demonstration of the comp in 4/4 and 3/4 on the downloaded recording "The Gypsy Swing Rhythm Comp."

As you listen to the full rhythm tracks, notice the difference in the way Jason Vanderford and I approach the comp. Jason's is very percussive, almost like a snare drum. I let my strums ring a little longer and you hear the notes of the chord a bit more. On mandolin I usually use chords with three notes, like the second G7 chord above, though occasionally I'll use four string chords that may or may not contain a root. The great mandolinist Jethro Burns suggested that the root can often be left out of a chord because the bass player usually supplies the root. If the bass player doesn't play it, the root is still implied and the audience doesn't miss it. Of course you'll need to carefully consider which notes you leave out. It's usually good to leave in the "flavor" notes of chords like modified sevens, thirds, fifths or ninths. Different combinations of notes will have different feels, color, and uses, and it's important for you to explore them all and see which you prefer in any given situation.

The mandolin I play on the recordings was built by the late Bob Schneider. It's a wonderful instrument, a kind of modified oval soundhole F4 of Bob's own design. It's got an incredibly rich, reverberant tone. It's pictured on the cover of this book and on page 107.

While it's true that the mandolin didn't play a major role in the initial history of Gypsy Swing in the 1930s, things began to change in the 1970s. The music of the David Grisman Quintet and others popularized the sounds of Gypsy Swing and inspired generations of acoustic string players to explore the music and make it part of their own repertoires. Mandolinists all over the world began learning the chords and melodies, joining swing, jazz, and Gypsy Swing bands, and trying to play the solos that Django and Stephane played so beautifully. Over the years we've seen that mandolinists can play wonderful, exciting, and inspiring rhythm and leads, just like the guitarists and fiddlers. So let's get swingin'!

Django Reinhardt

Avalon

"Avalon" has been played so much over the decades that it's known as a "standard." Standards are songs that are recognized and appreciated by succeeding generations of audiences. That's why musicians play them. "Avalon" is from what's called "The Great American Songbook." These are songs by American composers dating from the late 1910s through at least the 1960s.

The melody to "Avalon" is made up primarily of half notes and played at a quick tempo. The effect is to make the accompaniment sound as if it's in double time. The four measure string bass introduction is similar to one on a recording of "Avalon" by Django Reinhardt and Stephane Grappelli with the Quintette of the Hot Club of France. Occasionally an introduction is added to a song form. In this case, the string bass plays unaccompanied one time, at the very beginning of the tune. It's important to be able to recognize an intro as separate from the song and know where the intro ends and the form of the song begins.

I added some substitute chords in parentheses in measures nine through twelve. When a chord progression stays on a five dominant (V) chord, in this case a C7, for several measures, we can often swap in a two minor seven chord (ii m7), a Gm7 here. Try this alternate progression and see if you like it. You could also plug these changes in at measures one through four. Identify other extended passages of dominant seven chords in this and other songs and experiment with substituting the dominant seven's relative ii m7 chord.

The ending we recorded is a common and fun Hot Club/traditional jazz-style ending. The band stops after an accented break on beat one of the F (or "one" or Roman numeral "I") chord of measure thirty-one of the last chorus. After that I continue by sliding a tremoloed chord form up the guitar fingerboard from C to F to end on a last hit with the band. Try using the third C7 below and sliding it up to the first F chord shown to do something similar on the mandolin.

By the way, the lyrics to all the songs are included. Even if you're not a singer, it's important to know a song by its lyrics. I often have them running in my head as I play a melody or compose a solo. It helps me stay grounded on each specific song. The cadence of the lyrics and the way a singer phrases them can be a great source of inspiration in your own improvisations. Once you've memorized the melody as written, try moving it up an octave. Here's the melody moved up an octave and written out: **musixnow.com/avalon-gypsy-mando2-8va-score/**

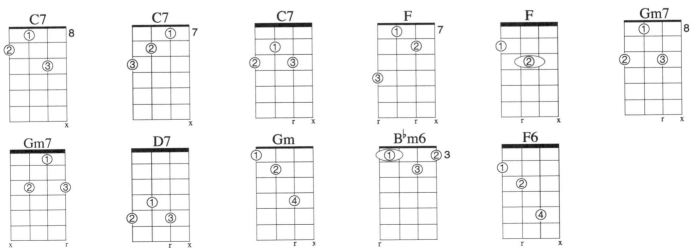

Avalon

Key of F

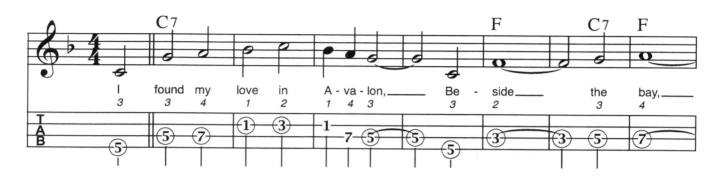

Jolson and Rose, 1920

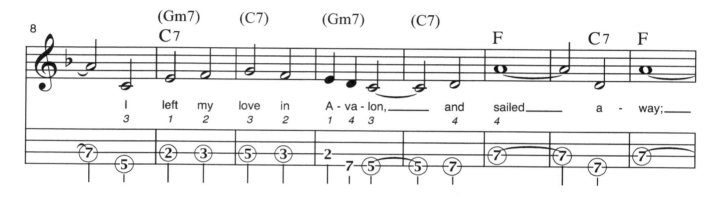

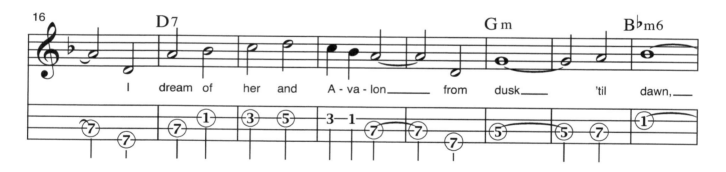

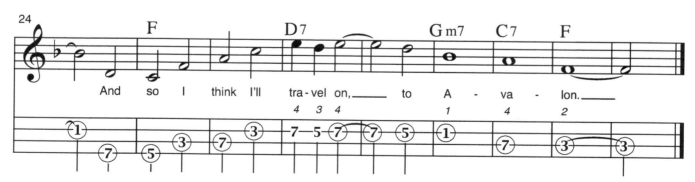

Arrangement © 2007 by Dix Bruce • Dix Bruce Music (BMI) • www.musixnow.com

Some of These Days

"Some of These Days" is a favorite of Red Hot Mama singers the world over. One of its interesting aspects is that it modulates between the keys of E minor and G major. E minor is the relative minor of G; G is the relative major of E minor and they share almost the same scale and key signature. See the note on major and minor scales on page 29.

I've listed alternate voicings for some of the chords below, notably the B7 and Em. You'll decide which to use by its sound or how it fits with the chords preceding and following. Try to compile sets of chords that don't require big jumps on the fingerboard. Many of these changes require that you move only one note to go from chord to chord. Explore these tight voicings and practice sets of changes that need only minimal fretting hand shifts. Feel free to bring in your own chord voicings or voicings from other songs in the book. The bottom line will always be sound and you may decide to use forms that require wide hand movements.

On the recording I diverge a bit here and there from the straight rhythm and add accents and counter rhythms on guitar. Django would often add little rhythmic flourishes like these behind Stephane's solos. When I add rhythmic variations I try to keep them to a minimum so they won't detract from the groove or compete with what the soloist is playing. Try accents like these on the mandolin with different voicings of the same chord.

The melody has a lot of chromatic tones in it as you can see from all the accidentals (sharps and flats) in the music. As a result, the suggested fingerings shift around a bit and you won't always play the same note at the same fret with the same finger. If you find the given fretting finger suggestions difficult, experiment with your own fingerings and positions.

After you can play the melody as written, move all the open second string A notes to the third string seventh fret. Move the open first string E notes to the second string seventh fret. It'll be good for you, I promise!

I took liberties with the melody, especially on the up-to-speed recording. I tried to "swingify" it a bit by adding a few more notes, some slides, and some rhythmic changes. I wanted it to be more alive and intense than a strict reading of the written melody would be. Is this legal? You bet it is! Not only are we jazz musicians, we are **mandolinic jazz musicians**. We live to do this!

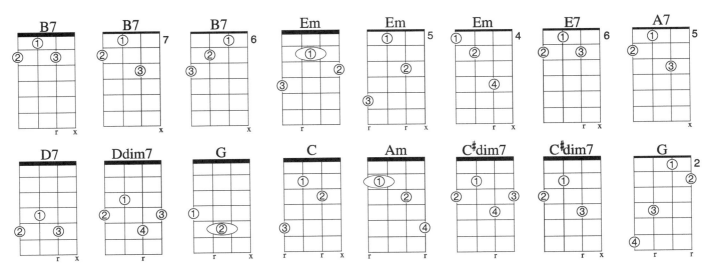

Some of These Days

Key of Em, G

Sheldon Brooks, 1910

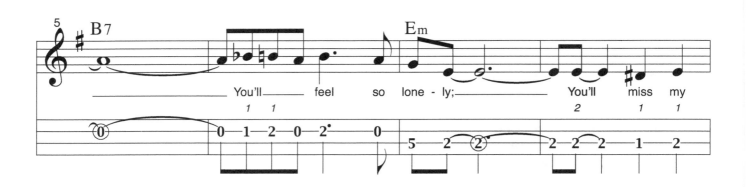

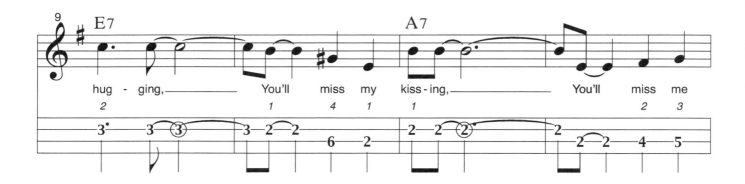

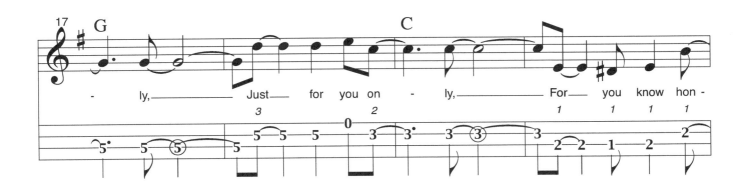

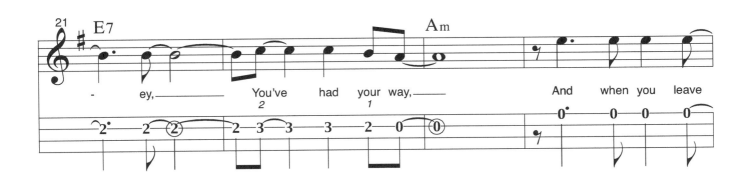

After You've Gone

"After You've Gone" is another great standard played by jazz musicians *everywhere*! It's a bit unusual in that the first chord of measure one is a IV ("four chord") in this case an F. Seeing F as the first chord might lead you to conclude that the song is in the key of F when it's actually in the key of C. The foolproof way to know what key a piece is in is to look at the key signature, the space between the treble clef sign and time signature on the left hand side of the music. The number of sharps or flats will define the key.

The example above from "Avalon" (page fourteen) has one flat in its key signature and that means that the song is in the key of F, even though the first chord is a C7. If there are no sharps or flats in the key signature, which is the case with "After You've Gone," the piece is in the key of C. For more info on the number of sharps and flats in keys, see the *Scale, Chord, and Transposition Chart* on page 74. Another fairly reliable method for determining the key of a piece is to find what chord the song ends on. If it ends on a C chord, the piece is probably in the key of C. If it ends on a Bb chord, then it's most likely in the key of Bb. If it ends on a Dm chord, the piece is probably in D minor. There are exceptions, but they're rare in pop music and jazz.

Again, I didn't play the up-to-speed melody exactly as written but added a few slides and rhythmic syncopations here and there when I recorded it. This is typical of a jazz interpretation of a melody. You can use this type of interpretation to compose melody-based or "rhythmized" solos.

We played a stop or "break" in the rhythm track at measure thirteen on the last time through. I kept a rhythm click going on the guitar to guide you. Having a break like this is a very common tool that musicians use to add interest and excitement to a performance. As a player you need to be able to count the rhythm in your head and not loose the groove. This break will give you practice counting.

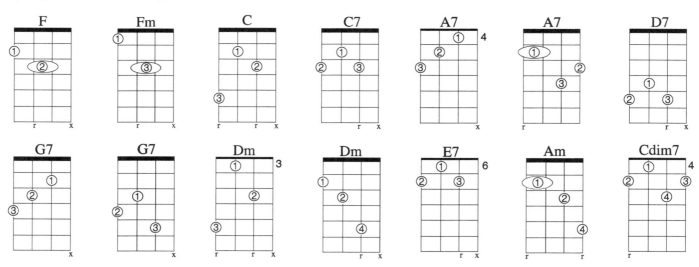

After You've Gone

Key of C

Creamer and Layton, 1918

Baby Won't You Please Come Home?

"Baby Won't You Please Come Home?" is in the key of Eb. If you're not used to it, playing in flat keys like Eb, Bb, Ab, etc., can strike fear into your heart. Once you've had experience playing in different keys, you'll find that one key is pretty much the same as any other. To play swing and jazz, it's important that you reach that point. Different players and especially different singers, will want to perform songs in different keys. For example, a horn player might like flat keys like F, Bb, Eb, etc., or a singer may need to move "Baby Won't You Please Come Home" from Eb to the key of C or G. Since the singer can't adjust his or her range, you need to adjust what you play to where they need to sing. Be prepared! Don't shy away from keys and sets of chords that you might find initially challenging. Practice moving all the songs in this book to a variety of other keys. The *Scale, Chord, and Transposition Chart* on page 74 will show you how to transpose any set of chords to any key.

The tablature to "Baby Won't You Please Come Home?" includes some open-string notes. After you can play the melody as written, try moving the open-string notes to closed, fretted positions.

"Baby Won't You Please Come Home" has an unusual form: it's eighteen measures in length. Most of the other songs in this book and in the jazz / pop repertoire are built on sixteen or thirty-two bar forms. "Baby Won't You Please Come Home" has two additional bars that include a built in "I really mean it!" Here's where the singer drops to one knee and really "sells" the song.

The last two measures of the last chorus of the rhythm track are extended. Instead of playing two beats each of the F7 and Bb7 chords, we play four beats or one whole measure of each. There are several types of extended and special endings like this in Gypsy Swing and Jazz and we'll explore a few of them in this book.

The first four notes of measure eleven are written as F, Eb, F, Eb. Some players prefer F, E, F, E. I recorded F, E, F, E on the slow and F, Eb, F, Eb on the up-to-speed recording.

Below you'll see additional forms of the G7, Bb7, Cm, and Ab chords. The different forms are interchangeable though each has a unique sound. Try using the form that's closest on the fingerboard to the chords that occur before and after to avoid an awkward hand shift.

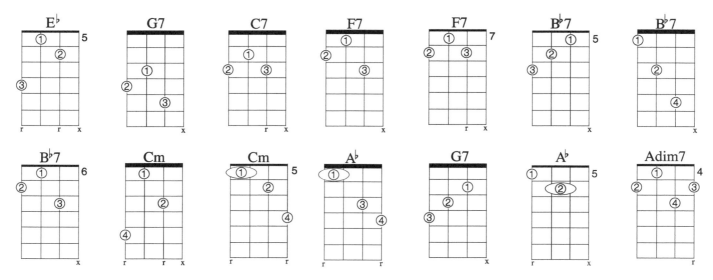

Baby Won't You Please Come Home?

Key of Eb

C. Williams and C. Warfield, 1919

Swing in Minor

"Swing in Minor" is based on a Reinhardt and Grappelli composition called "Minor Swing." They recorded it several times in the key of Am, so that's where "Swing in Minor" is set. David Grisman recorded a wonderful arrangement of "Minor Swing" in the late 1970s in the key of Dm. Grisman's uses Django and Stephane's second "head" (discussed below) as the melody to his version. Check out the Dm version of "Swing in Minor" on page 24. You can use the melodies to "Swing in Minor" in either key as a solo over the chord changes to "Minor Swing."

"Swing in Minor" has a somewhat unusual form with two different melodies or "heads." One is played at the beginning of the tune, one at the end. We've edited the two together on the recording so you can practice both. As you'll hear, both are punctuated by band breaks or stops with fills by the string bass. Since the band plays one whole note in every measure in the first part it is incumbent on the soloist to provide very clear swing rhythm structure and timing in their lead.

The mandolin harmonics played at the end of the up-to-speed melody are played at the twelfth fret on strings one and two. To play a harmonic, lay a fretting finger lightly on the string pair over the fret wire, in this case the twelfth. Don't press down but pick the string as usual. Make sure you're above the fret wire, not the fret space. Work toward getting a chime-like sound.

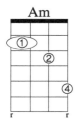
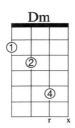
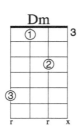
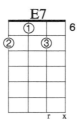
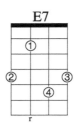
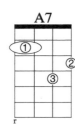

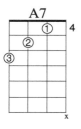
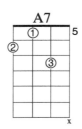

Chords for the key of Dm version on page 24:

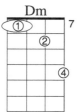
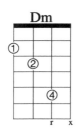
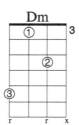
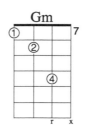
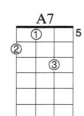
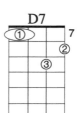
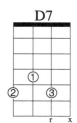

Swing in Minor

Key of Am

Dix Bruce, 2007

Swing in Minor

Key of Dm

In melody:

Dix Bruce, 2007

Chicago

"Chicago" has been a jazz standard since it was introduced in the early 1920s. It was written by the great Fred Fisher, who also wrote "Peg o' My Heart," "Dardanella," "Daddy, You've Been a Mother to Me," and "Your Feet's Too Big." "Chicago" has a slightly unusual form where only the first four measures are repeated. The melody is built around a repetitive syncopated rhythmic riff. You'll hear it again and again with the lyrics "Chi-ca-go, Chi-ca-go." As you work through the melody, try to get that same swing and bounce. You'll notice that I significantly "rhythmized" or "swingified" the fast version of the melody. The rhythm just seemed to demand it.

Lots and lots of chords in the accompaniment department! They're all great forms that you'll use again and again in this style of music. In some cases I gave you more than one form to choose from.

We added a break in the rhythm after the first chorus. Jason plays a rhythm click during the break to keep the band honest, rhythm-wise. In a real life band situation, probably only the soloist would be playing here. You need to keep the rhythm in your head and come in at the right time at the top of the next chorus.

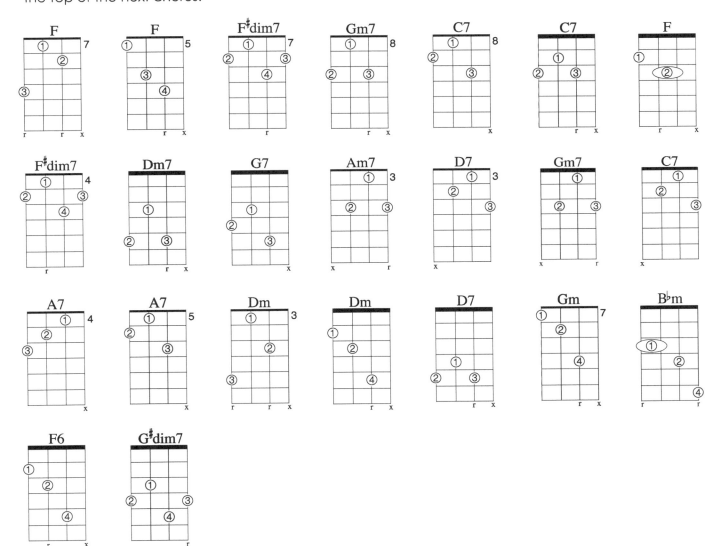

Chicago

Key of F

F. Fisher, 1922

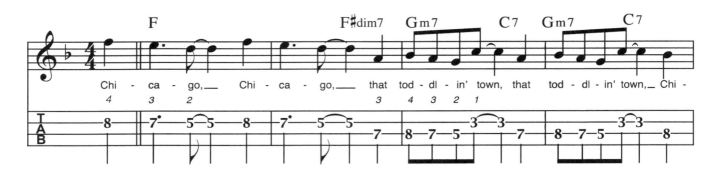

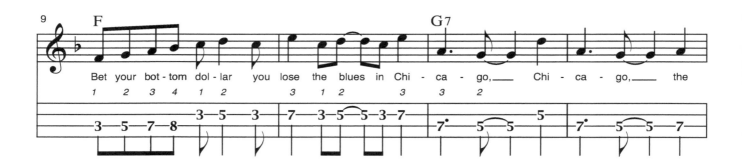

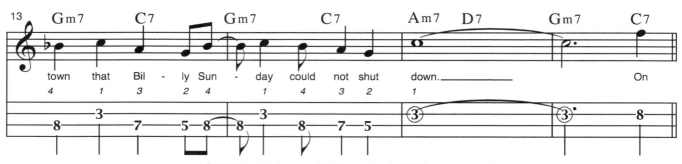

Arrangement © 2007 by Dix Bruce • Dix Bruce Music (BMI) • www.musixnow.com

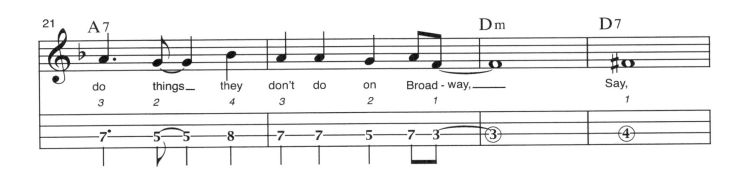

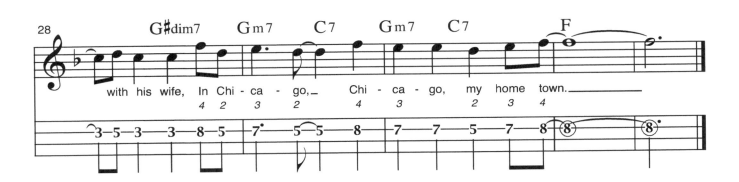

St. Louis Blues

"St. Louis Blues" was written by W.C. Handy in 1914 and was one of the first blues compositions to become a huge international hit. It's been a standard of musicians all over the world, especially jazz players, for over one hundred years. It's still played everywhere.

Blues has been called the father of jazz and if you want to understand jazz you need to be familiar with the blues. The blues form is relatively simple and built on a twelve measure pattern: one measure of the I chord (in this case G), one of the IV (C), two of the I (G or G7), two of the IV (C or C7), two of the I, two of the V (D7), two of the I. Not every blues has these exact chords in this exact order. Often you'll encounter variations. One of the interesting things about "St. Louis Blues" is that it combines a G major blues progression with a sixteen measure G minor bridge or middle section in a Latin rhythm. It's usually referred to as a tango, but some people call it an *habanera*. This minor/Latin part is only played once, during the initial statement of the melody, sandwiched between two sets of major blues chord changes. The solos are played over the twelve bar major blues chord changes.

Like many of the songs in this book, the melody to "St. Louis Blues" is written with some open-string notes. Play it first as written with open-string notes, then re-locate these open notes to fretted positions and play the melody there. It's important for you to learn all these melodies in closed position without open strings. You can download a closed-position version of "St. Louis Blues" from my website: **musixnow.com/wp-content/uploads/St.Louisgypsymclosed.pdf**

One of the secrets to making your solos sound bluesy is to add "blue notes" to them. The blue notes I use most often are the flatted third and the flatted seventh tones of the scale. For "St. Louis Blues" in the key of G, these blue notes would be Bb and F natural. See the scales below.

G major scale

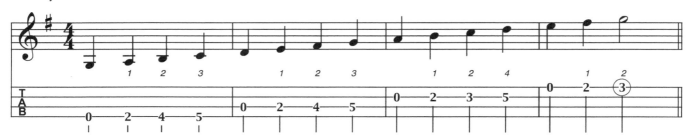

G major scale with blue notes: flatted third and seventh notes

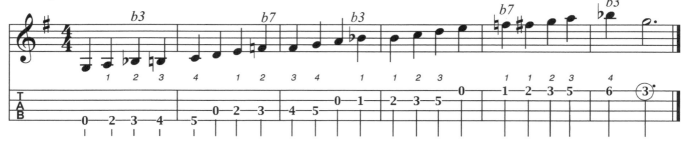

Most songs have a home tonality and a lot of the interest in a melody or solo comes from moving away from and coming back to this tonality or "home." Blue notes provide tension as they work against the home tonality. Once a tonality is stated, your ear expects to hear the regular third and seventh tones. In "St. Louis Blues" in the key of G major, those notes are B and F#. When you add the Bb and F natural notes, it's somewhat unexpected and interesting. Try adding the Bb and F natural tones to your "St. Louis Blues" solos in the key of G. Make sure they reference the root of your home tonality, in this case G, and resolve or come back to that note often.

The bridge in Gm is a whole different animal. Here you can use *most* of the notes of the G major scale with the flatted third and seventh tones, but you'll probably want to avoid the notes B natural and F#, especially over the Gm chord. Those notes are not part of the Gm scale. They would definitely add tension but not quite the right kind for blues.

But there's more. In order to have a V or dominant seven chord in G minor, a D7, we need an F# note since the D7 chord includes the notes D – F# – A – C. When we change the F natural in the Gm scale to the F#, we create the G *harmonic minor scale*. It looks like this:

G harmonic minor scale with raised 7th notes (F#)

When you're deciding which notes to play, always consider the underlying chord. Chord tones will always sound "good." Since the Gm chord includes the notes G – Bb – D, those notes will fit perfectly when played over the Gm chord. The other notes of the G harmonic scale will generally work as passing tones, that is, as notes played on your way to chord tones. The longer you stay on these notes, the more discordant they can seem as they clash with the chord tones. Likewise the D7 chord tones, the notes D – F# – A – C, will fit well over the D7 chord.

Be sure to work out different closed-position versions of these scales. Figure out each scale with your first fretting finger playing the root on the fourth string. Then try a different position with your second fretting finger playing the root and so on through the positions where your third and fourth fretting fingers play the root. Some may not be possible without hand shifts. This exercise will help you learn where these notes are located on the fingerboard. Try moving all the scales to other keys.

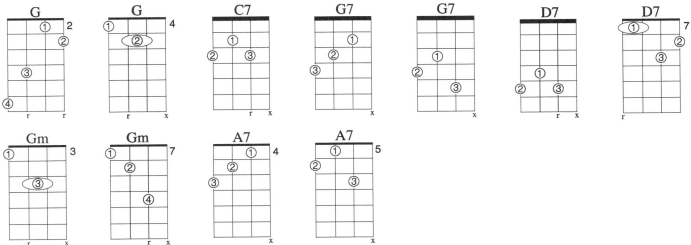

St. Louis Blues

Key of G, Gm

W.C. Handy, 1914

Arrangement © 2007 by Dix Bruce • Dix Bruce Music (BMI) • www.musixnow.com

The Sheik of Araby

"The Sheik of Araby" first appeared in 1921 and has been a popular standard ever since. I've usually played in the key of Bb, which is where I've written it below. The melody is a combination of staccato and legato notes with a repetitive rhythmic motif: quarter notes followed by dotted halves.

As mentioned in the introduction, most of the melodies and chords in this book are written in closed position with no open-string notes. The great advantage of learning a melody, solo, or chords in a closed position is that you can easily move them up or down the mandolin fingerboard to different keys. For example, once you have the chord progression or melody to "The Sheik" memorized, move it up in pitch two frets and you'll be in the key of C. In "The Sheik of Araby" you'll find several seventh fret third string A notes (measures eight, nine, fourteen, twenty eight and twenty nine) played with the fourth finger. You *could* play these A notes on the open second string but then you wouldn't have a closed-position moveable melody.

Because the mandolin is tuned in fifths, that is, the interval between any two adjacent strings is a perfect fifth, melodies can also be moved *across* as well as up and down the fingerboard. This gives you another way to transpose a melody to a different key. When you've memorized the first, lower octave version of "The Sheik" on page 33, try moving it "over" one string so that your first note is on the third fret of string four. Keep the relative positions of the other notes in tact and you'll move the melody to the key of Eb. After that, try the upper octave version on page 34. In this example we'll stay in the key of Bb and move the melody up a full octave. As you'll see, your fingerings will be exactly the same as in the lower octave version though on different strings. Try these types of modulations on every melody. If a melody has open-string notes, move them to a fretted position.

For the longer, sustained notes in "The Sheik" and other songs in this set, I used tremolo, especially on the slower versions. Without it, the notes decay quite quickly. I like the extra sustain that tremolo allows. The difficulty can be in getting the tremolo started and then controlling it to end where you want it to end cleanly. It's good to practice starting and stopping your tremolo. Whether you use tremolo or not is ultimately an artistic decision. You could just as easily play "The Sheik" without any tremolo at all or only on selected notes.

The ending is one of those "chord tremolo windup, take no prisoners, the song is over, now go home" type of things. Remember: it's always nice when the band ends together!

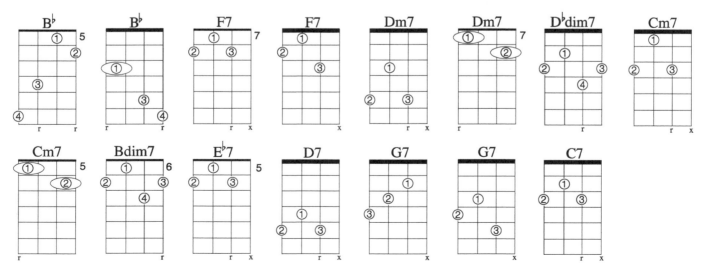

The Sheik of Araby

Key of Bb

T. Snyder, H. Smith, and F. Wheeler, 1921

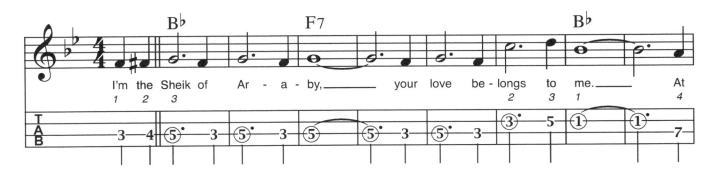

I'm the Sheik of Ar - a - by,_____ your love be - longs to me._____ At

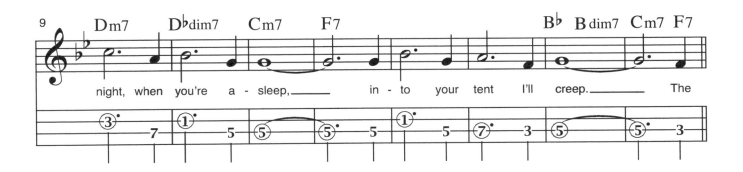

night, when you're a - sleep,_____ in - to your tent I'll creep._____ The

stars that shine a - bove,_____ will light our way to love,_____ you'll

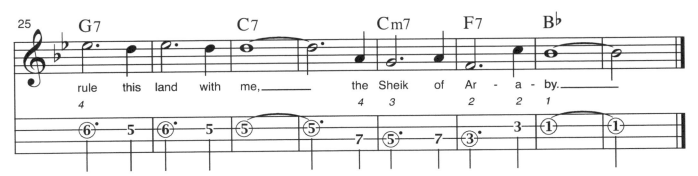

rule this land with me,_____ the Sheik of Ar - a - by.

The Sheik of Araby transposed up an octave:

China Boy

"China Boy" has a relatively simple and straight forward legato melody with lots of long, flowing, sustained notes. It starts out in the key of F but modulates to the key of Ab, up a minor third, in measure sixteen with the Eb7 chord. The song stays in Ab until measure twenty-four where the C7 chord, the V chord of the original key of F, moves it back to the key of F. The modulations give the song an interesting ebb and flow. They also necessitate two quite different fretting hand positions which are reflected in the tablature and fretting hand finger suggestions.

On the track I play the melody very close to the way it's written with some syncopations and anticipations to swing it up a bit. You don't necessarily want to play these melodies exactly as written. Add your own swing and jazz phrasing. If you're not sure what this means, spend some time listening to Django and Stephane and compare what they do to the written versions of these songs.

The melody to "China Boy" has no open-string notes, they're all fretted and located on strings two and three. That makes it a great candidate to move "over" one string and transpose the melody to a new key. Try playing your first note on the seventh fret of string four. Keep the relative note positions the same and play them on strings three and four instead of strings two and three. (You'll play the same TAB numbers on different strings and be in the key of Bb.) Once you can do that, try playing your first note on the seventh fret of string two. All your notes will be on strings one and two and you will have transposed "China Boy" to the key of C. Again, play the same relative note positions. You can also move any of these positions *up* the fingerboard. For example, start the original melody on string three, fret nine to transpose the melody to the key of G.

The slow version of the melody on the recording has no tremolo, the up-to-speed melody does. Try it both ways and see which you prefer.

At about 2:04 into the band track I add a rhythm riff on the guitar. I picked a riff that fit with what Jason Vanderford and Steve Hanson (guitar and bass respectively) were playing and worked it again and again through the changes and up to the modulation where I reverted to regular rhythm. Then I went back to the rhythm riff for the last eight measures of the key of F part. I do a similar rhythm riff on mandolin in the last chorus, which begins about 3:00. The ending to the track has another typical Django-esque windup and abrupt ending.

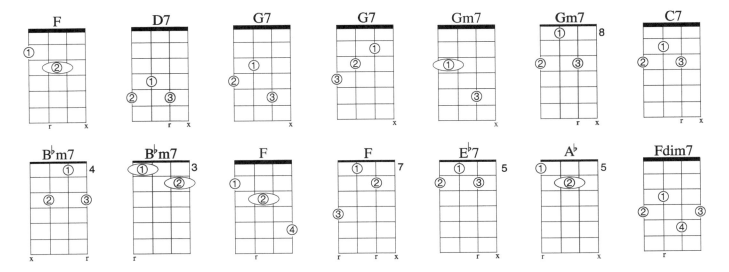

China Boy

Key of F

D. Winfree and P. Boutelje, 1922

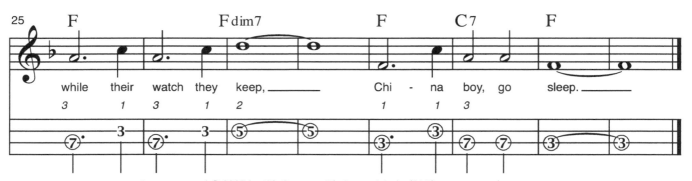

Rose Room

"Rose Room" dates back to 1914 and was a popular song that became an early jazz standard. Duke Ellington's "In a Mellow Tone" uses the same chord changes.

If you find the key of Ab difficult, it's probably because you haven't played in this key much. As I've mentioned, it's important that you be able to play in all keys. The Quintette recorded "Rose Room" in the key of F but every band I've played with does it in Ab. Since we already have so many songs in F, and nothing so far in Ab, I decided to arrange "Rose Room" in Ab. With a little bit of work, you, as a mandolinist, can transpose any song to any key. As you did with "China Boy," move the closed melody "down" one string so your first note is on the fourth string, first fret. You'll be in the key of Db. Once you've mastered that, move both positions up the fingerboard. Remember to relocate that lone open-string note in measure thirteen to a closed position!

Jason Vanderford plays a simple four-bar introduction that lands on the Eb7 or V chord of the key of Ab. You can clearly hear his comping style here — very rhythmic. He reduces the sound of his chord to where it's barely more than a click. Like many of the Gypsy Swing players he uses a very thick pick that I'd guess is over an 1/8 inch thick. He's acting as a drummer and concentrating on the back beat. It is typical in Hot Club-style rhythm sections to have more than one rhythm player comping all the time. Django and Stephane usually had two rhythm guitarists in addition to whatever rhythm Django played. Listen to how beautifully they work together. With multiple rhythm players there can be a danger of actually diluting the groove if all the musicians aren't playing together. Everyone has to be playing the same type of rhythm at the same time, and it helps for each player to pull back a bit and serve the band's groove and the soloist. In these cases less is more.

In measures seven through ten the chord progression moves from Db to Dbm, or from IV ("four") to iv ("four minor"). Some players change to the Dbm in measure nine. In this version we change to the Dbm in measure ten. At the end of the first chorus, the band breaks on the first beat of the last two Ab measures. Again, I keep a rhythmic click going so we don't lose the groove. This type of break, prevalent in all styles of swing and jazz, gives the first soloist an extra two bars to launch into and set up the solo.

On the mandolin we have the choice of using tremolo to extend notes. To demonstrate I used tremolo on the slow recording of the melody but not on the fast so you can hear the differences.

I recently played a gig where the band performed "Rose Room" as a tango. Give it a try!

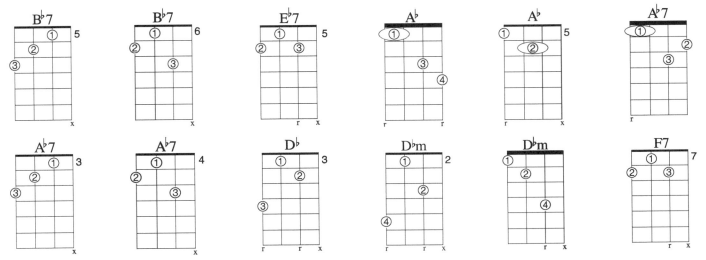

Rose Room

Key of Ab

A. Hickman and H. Williams, 1917

Dark Eyes

"Dark Eyes" is probably Russian in origin, certainly Eastern European, and it's one of those songs that evokes wagons around a campfire, dancing and singing in a gypsy camp late into the night. It's loaded with potential for emotion and passion. Our version begins in 3/4 (page 40) and moves into 4/4 (page 41) with a six-measure transition. The transition begins with four measures of solo guitar chords, shown below with mandolin chords and tablature, to set up the new meter and tempo. Try playing it on the mandolin. The transition is followed with a two-measure solo bass fill by Steve Hanson. Solos can be played over either meter, but they're usually played over the 4/4 section, as we've done here. The lyrics are transliterated from the Russian. Regarding making up your own solos, see the note on the harmonic minor scale on page 29.

Transition chords:

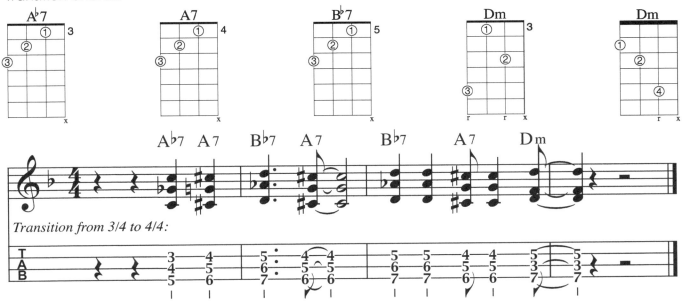

The ending to "Dark Eyes" has a repeat of the final four measures with a *ritard* or slow down on the repeat. If you decide to use this type of ending, be sure to warn your fellow players to expect such a thing. If you're the band leader, give clues and cues that something unexpected is about to happen and lead the change in rhythm. If you're a player, listen and watch closely and expect the unexpected.

"Dark Eyes" chords:

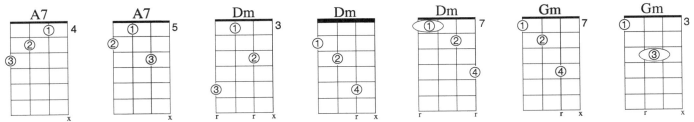

Dark Eyes

Key of Dm, 3/4 time

Traditional, Russian

O - tchi tchor - ny - ia, O - tchi - strast - ny - ia, O - tchi

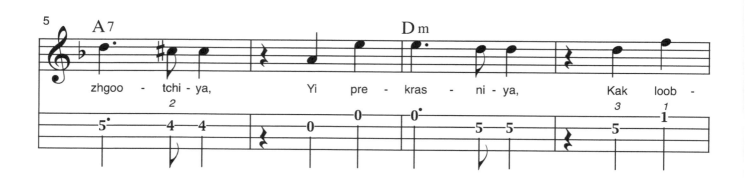

zhgoo - tchi - ya, Yi pre - kras - ni - ya, Kak loob -

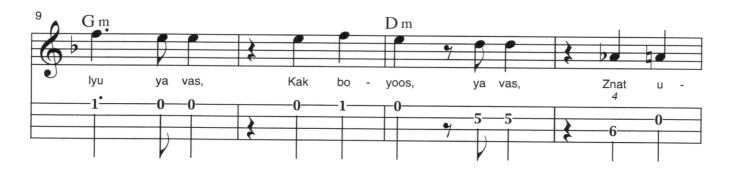

lyu ya vas, Kak bo - yoos, ya vas, Znat u -

vi - diel vas, Ya v'nie dobry tchas.

Dark Eyes

Key of Dm, 4/4 time

Traditional, Russian

Last time repeat last 4 bars twice, ritard last repeat.

Swingin' Like '42

"Swingin' Like '42" is based on a popular Reinhardt and Grappelli composition called "Swing 42." They also composed and recorded different tunes titled "Swing 39" and "Swing 48."

Generically speaking, "Swingin' Like '42" has what are called "rhythm changes." These are chord changes based on the 1930 George and Ira Gershwin song "I Got Rhythm" and literally thousands of other songs have these same changes. The classic chord changes are I ("one" C), vi ("six" Am), ii ("two" Dm), V ("five" G7), over and over again. Next to blues changes, "rhythm changes" with all their variations are probably the most prevalent chord progressions in pop music and jazz. Musicians on the bandstand often identify a song simply as "rhythm changes in C" or "rhythm changes in Ab." "Swingin' Like '42," which is in the key of C, has some additional changes and substitutions (minor seven chords for the regular minor chords) but is still considered "rhythm changes" or variations of I vi ii V. The song also modulates from the key of C to the key of E and back and uses the same progression I ("one" E), vi ("six" C#m), ii ("two" F#m), V ("five" B7) in the key of E.

I use the open fourth string G several times in the melody to "Swingin' Like '42" so it makes sense to me to use other open-string notes too. Since the lowest note in the melody is the lowest note on the mandolin, you can't transpose it to a lower key. Try transposing it up in pitch to other keys. I played a variation in measure seven on the up-to-speed recording. Can you figure it out?

Let's discuss chord numbering. The numbers are based on the notes of the scale of the home key of a song or passage. The first sixteen measures of "Swingin' Like '42" are in the key of C. How do we know that for sure? We can see that there are no sharps or flats in the key signature. (Look at the diagram on page 18 if you're not sure where to look to find the key signature.) If a song or passage is in the key of C, the chord numbers will be based on the C major scale. See the diagram below.

Scale:	C	D	E	F	G	A	B	C
Interval:		w	w	h	w	w	w	h
Note #:	1	2	3	4	5	6	7	8/1
Chord #:	I	ii	iii	IV	V	vi	vii°	VIII or I
Chords:	C	Dm	Em	F	G	Am	Bdim	C

The first line shows you the notes that make up the C major scale. The distances or "intervals" between notes in all major scales have a unique whole step (w) and half step (h) pattern shown in the second line. There are whole steps between notes 1 and 2, 2 and 3, 4 and 5, 5 and 6, 6 and 7, and half steps between notes 3 and 4 and 7 and 8. If you start on any note and follow this pattern, you'll play the major scale for that note.

The third line shows the scale number of each note in the major scale. Notes 1 and 8 are the same note an octave apart, and you could call note 8 a 1. When we refer to notes in a scale, we use Arabic numerals.

Chords derived from these notes are usually represented by Roman numerals. That's shown in the fourth line. Upper case Roman numerals denote major chords and lower case Roman numerals denote minor chords. The odd man out is the vii which has a little degree sign "°" after the number. The "°" symbol signifies a diminished chord. These three-note chords or "triads" use only the notes of the associated major scale. Chords with four or more notes, like D7, E7, or A7 in the key of C, use notes borrowed from other major scales. If we only use the notes from the associated major scale, the I, IV, and V chords are major; the iii, iii, and vi are minor; and the vii is diminished.

Find the space after measure ten on the right side of the staff on the following page. Suddenly there are four sharps in the key signature. That tells us that the song is changing key or modulating to a key with four sharps. That key is E major, which is diagrammed below.

E	F#	G#	A	B	C#	D#	E
w	w	h	w	w	w	h	
1	2	3	4	5	6	7	8/1
I	ii	iii	IV	V	vi	vii°	VIII or I
E	F#m	G#m	A	B	C#m	D#dim	E

The chords, even though they're in the key of E, still follow the general I-vi-ii-V number pattern.

What about that B7 in measure ten? Shouldn't it be a Bdim? This B7 is actually a borrowed chord. It belongs in the key of E and it's the V or dominant seven chord of the key of E. The B7 is being used as the transition chord between the keys of C and E. We often use the dominant seven chord of the key we're modulating *into* to facilitate a key change. We do the same thing in measure eighteen with the G7, the dominant seven chord of the key of C, to bring us back to the key of C. Notice the four natural signs on the staff after measure eighteen. These cancel the four sharps after measure ten. Dominant seven chords are used to facilitate modulations in "China Boy" on page 36. Find other songs in this book that use the dominant seven chord in the same way.

In the mid-1970s mandolinist and "dawg" music creator David Grisman often played "Swing 42" in his early Quintets. This popularized the tune among acoustic string jazz and bluegrass players, and it became a kind of standard in those genres. The melody to "Swingin' Like '42" will work as a solo on the chord changes of "Swing '42."

If you play "Swingin' Like '42" more than once through, use the chord changes from the first ending for the last two measures. These changes (C, C#dim7, Dm7, G7) will bring you back to the top of the form. Use the changes as written in the last two measures when you end the song.

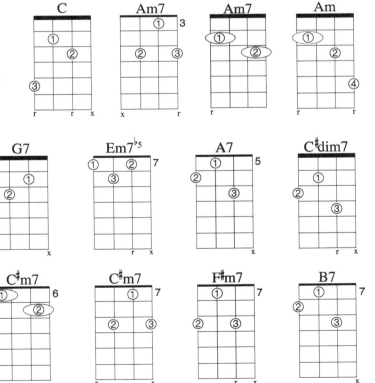

Swingin' Like '42

Key of C

Dix Bruce, 2007

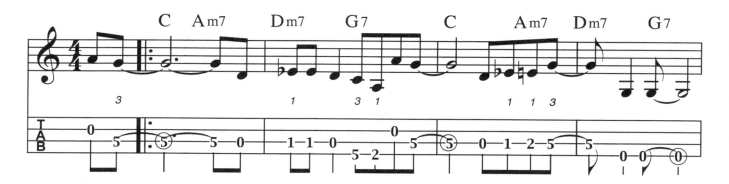

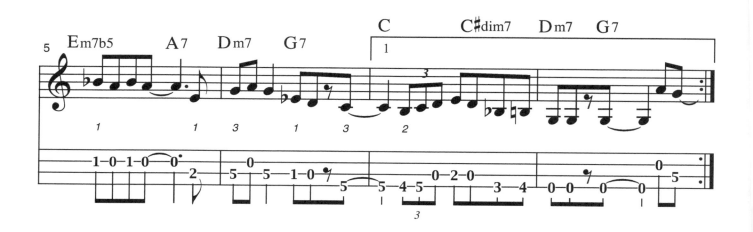

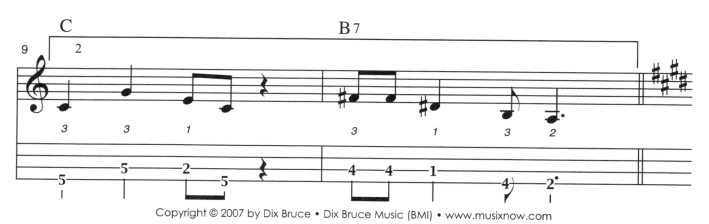

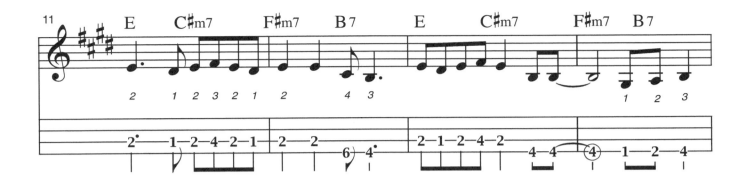

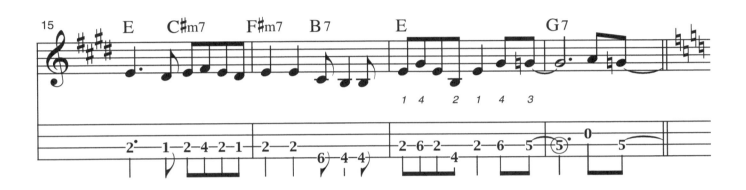

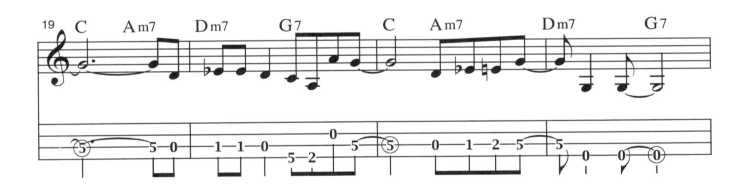

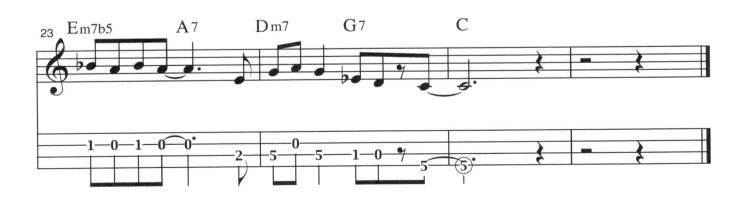

Limehouse Blues

"Limehouse Blues" has been a popular tune in jazz since the 1920s. Django Reinhardt and Stephane Grappelli recorded it at least twice together, once at a moderate tempo, once at a breakneck pace. The tempo of our recorded version, written in the key of G, is somewhere in between, tending toward the faster tempo. Once you learn a tune at a slower tempo, you can always speed it up.

"Limehouse Blues" is written in cut time, signified by a **C** in the time signature with a vertical line through it: **¢**. If there was no line and only a **C**, the meter would be "common time" or 4/4. Cut time means to give each note half its written value. So notes written as quarters are played as eighths, halves as quarters, effectively doubling the tempo of a piece. Cut time isn't always noted in the time signature; often it's just implied by the way a person counts off a tune: "One – two, one – two – three – four."

As you've read on previous pages, I always urge students to learn *everything* in closed positions without open-string notes. That's so you can easily shift a melody or chord progression to other keys up and down the fingerboard. Open-string notes make transposing much more difficult. The first version of "Limehouse Blues" is shown in the lower octave with some open-string notes. When you can play it from memory, learn the second version on page 48, this time closed, with no open-string notes. This closed melody can be moved up and down the fingerboard to different keys by simply shifting your relative fretting hand position. Work your way up the neck to an upper octave version of "Limehouse Blues" in the key of G. Your first note will be the seventh fret, second string E fretted with finger one. If you can't figure it out, download the music from my website: **musixnow.com/limehouse-blues-gypsy-mando8va/** Move all the melodies in this book around to new keys and also to find lower or higher octave versions of your melodies and solos. Doing so will help you discover the secrets of the mystic fingerboard!

The first chord is a C9, a C7 with a D note, the "nine" of the C scale, added. A dominant nine chord can often be used as a substitution for a dominant seven and vice versa. We could also substitute dominant nine chords for the other dominant sevens in "Limehouse Blues," A9 for A7, D9 for D7, etc. B9 for B7 going into Em may not work as there are other issues to consider, e.g., the nine of the B7 is C#, which is not in the Em or G scale. Perhaps we can get to that in another book. Also try substituting the G6 for the regular G I ("one") chord.

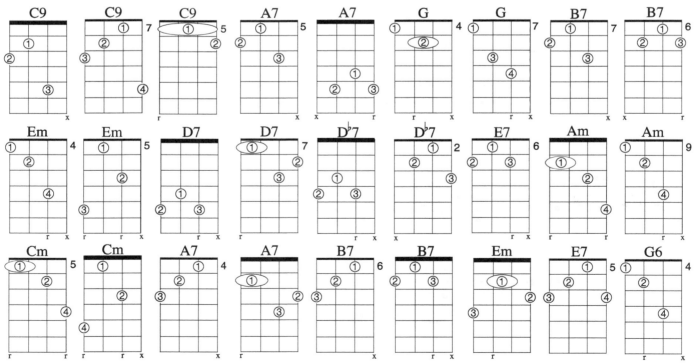

Limehouse Blues

Key of G

Braham and Furber, 1922

Limehouse Blues closed position

Chinatown, My Chinatown

In "Chinatown, My Chinatown" we'll work through a few exercises that I've suggested you explore with all the songs in this book. The melody is written in a lower octave, closed position, on frets two through seven. When you can play it from memory, try figuring out the same melody an octave higher, starting on the first string, eighth fret C note. I've posted the music and TAB on my web site if you need it, but you'll learn a whole lot more if you work through it on your own. Compared to guitar, the mandolin makes moving a melody up or down an octave or to other keys relatively easy. Because the mandolin is tuned in intervals of fifths that makes patterns consistent from string to string. Use the online music to check what you come up with. Here's the link: **musixnow.com/gypsyswing2downloads**.

There's a two measure/eight beat break in the rhythm on the band track at the end of the melody and before the first solo. As you've seen previously in this book, jazz musicians do this frequently to highlight the change from playing the melody to playing solos. On other breaks on the recordings we keep a click going on rhythm guitar so everybody clearly knows where to come back in. We left it out here to give you practice counting, or better yet, feeling the rhythm.

In the third chorus of the band track, about 1:08 into the cut, I play a simple and syncopated rhythmic riff, mostly with higher position chords on the guitar, which I carry through to the end of the chorus. (See page 62 for more about "choruses.") The riff adds some extra texture to the back up during that chorus. I always take care when doing this type of thing as there's a danger of goofing up the rhythm and destroying the main pulse. On the classic recordings of the Hot Club, Django and Stephane played over two rhythm guitars and string bass. When Stephane played, Django often added little rhythmic bits and flourishes like this on top of the regular rhythm. We hear these brilliant chordal accents that Django played and, of course, we want to play them too. The trick is to do it when you have a solid rhythm section behind you and to not play too much. Be subtle and always consider how what you play affects the main rhythmic groove and the lead. You should never compete with either, and always play something that makes the groove stronger. I can't recall an instance where Stephane played back up behind Django. He may have but it was certainly rare.

Many of the melodies for the accompanying audio were played fairly close to the way they're written and without much variation, especially on the slow recordings. When I play these same melodies at a jam session or in performance, I take liberties to make the music swing. I may add or subtract notes, accent them differently, or "rhythmize" the basic melody. I added pickups and rhythmized the melody on "Chinatown, My Chinatown.""Rhythmization," which we'll also explore with "Whispering" on page 62, involves staying very close to the pitches of a given melody but with modified rhythms and a few added notes. After you've memorized the melody, try rhythmizing it in your own way. Rhythmization is a great way to develop a solo that stays close to the melody. You can always take off from there and add in as many melodic and rhythmic ideas as you want. By the way, older jazz musicians often describe the process of improvisation in jazz as "take off."

Another exercise to try on "Chinatown, My Chinatown" is to play the melody with octaves. Django often used octaves to give his melodies and solos an added intensity. This song is a good candidate for octaves because the melody doesn't have a lot of eighth note or faster passages. When playing octaves on the mandolin, your hand will jump around quite a bit. Longer notes and medium tempos will give you a fighting chance to use the technique!

I play all the upper notes of the octave with the fourth finger, the lower notes with the first. Octave pairs on the mandolin are played on strings one and two, two and three, and three and four. Pairs of octave notes will have four "open" frets between them. Your fretted octave notes will span six frets. It can take some time to learn to play octaves smoothly, but the result is well worth the effort.

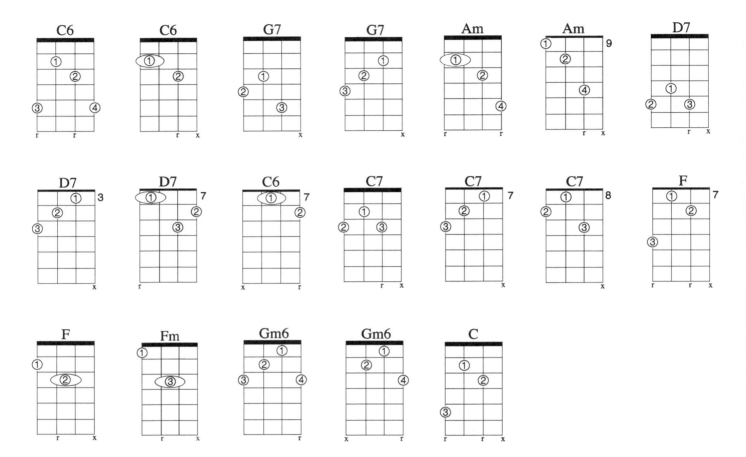

Dix Bruce's Swing & Jazz Mandolin: Chords, Rhythm, & Songs
(DVD) Learn at your own pace as Dix takes you through all the basics, including the swing/jazz rhythm comp, turnarounds, music theory, diminished chords, transposing, basic chord substitutions, common swing/jazz chord progressions, and more. Play along and learn each chord progression at both slow and regular speed. Over 100 minutes of video instruction! Build a repertoire of moveable chords while learning eight great songs played by swing/jazz musicians all over the world. See our mandolin products page: **musixnow.com/books-mandolin/**

Chinatown, My Chinatown

Key of C

Jerome and Schwartz 1910

St. James Infirmary

"St. James Infirmary" is an old minor blues that looms large in the legend of New Orleans music. I've always found it to be a chilling and moving tale. Django recorded an amazingly melancholy version of it in 1950 with a jazz band.

The form of "St. James Infirmary" is only eight measures long. On the recordings of the melody, we stretched it to sixteen. The first part demonstrates the melody in a lower octave and the second part shows the same thing an octave higher. The lower octave version has some open-string notes, the upper octave version is in closed position with no open-string notes. Notice that the open-string notes offer different timbres than the fretted notes. They're all colors for our musical paintbox and we need to be familiar with the possibilities each different sound offers. After you've memorized the lower melody as written, substitute fretted notes for all the open-stringed notes. Try to move the upper closed-position melody over two strings and down an octave. Your first note will be at the seventh fret of string four, played with the first finger.

You can substitute a Bb6 for the Gm7 chords. The Bb6 has the same notes as the Gm7. Try substituting both the Bb6 and Gm7 forms for the Gm.

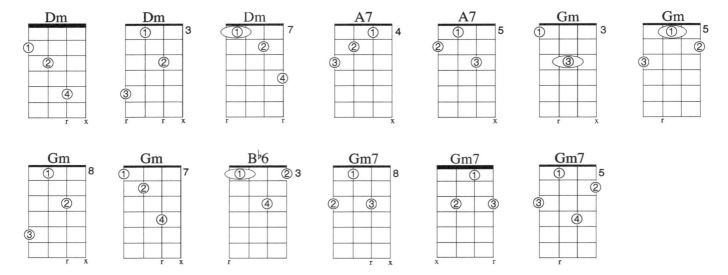

Additional lyrics:

3. I was down to St. James Infirmary,
And I saw my baby there,
She was stretched out on a long white table,
So cold, so clean, so fair.

4. Let her go, let her go, God bless her,
Wherever she may be,
She may search this wide world over,
But she'll never find a sweet, loving man like me.

5. Now when I die dress me up and bury me,
A box-back coat and a Stetson hat,
Put a twenty-dollar gold piece on my watch chain,
So the boys'll know I died standing pat.

6. I want six crap shooters for my pallbearers,
And a chorus girl to sing me a song,
Put a jazz band on my hearse wagon,
Just to raise hell as we roll along.

7. You can carry me down to the graveyard,
Six black horses and rubber-tired hack,
There'll be thirteen good men that go down there,
But there ain't but twelve coming back.

8. Now that you've heard my story,
I'll take another shot of booze,
If anyone should happen to ask you,
Say I've got the gambler's blues.

St. James Infirmary

Key of Dm

Traditional

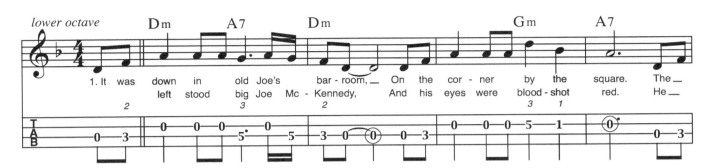

1. It was down in old Joe's bar-room, On the cor-ner by the square. The —
   left stood big Joe Mc-Kennedy, And his eyes were blood-shot red. He —

drinks were served as usu-al, And the usu-al crowd was there. — 2. On my
looked at the gang a-round him, — And these were the words he said. —

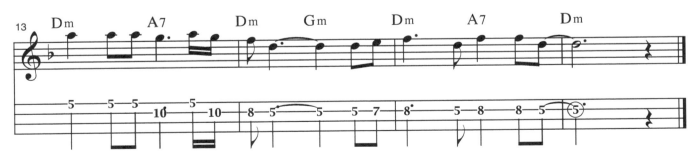

Clouds and Shadows

We tend to think of the music of the Quintette of the Hot Club of France and Gypsy Swing music in general as hot, fast, and passionate. It's no wonder since Django Reinhardt and Stephane Grappelli recorded some of the hottest, fastest, swingingest music in history. But they also played many slow and beautiful ballads. One of Django's most famous and celebrated compositions is the stunning "Nuages," which he recorded at least seventeen times, both solo and with a variety of musical accompaniment. "Clouds and Shadows" is a melody I wrote to a chord progression similar to "Nuages," the French word for "clouds." Once you memorize it, you can use it as an alternate melody or solo to "Nuages."

The chord progression to "Clouds and Shadows" includes some surprises, chords we might not have seen previously such as the Am7b5 or the Cm6, or unanticipated chords in the key of G, like the Eb7 and the Ab7. The Eb7 works like a raised dominant V chord. The expected V in the key of G would be the D7. In measures three, eight, nineteen, and thirty-one you'll see a G6 chord. Even though this is not reflected in the melody, the accompaniment musicians should play a G6.

Don't be intimidated by all the chords shown on this or other songs. I wanted to give you two or three choices for each so that you'd experiment with the sounds and evaluate the ease of playing each with other surrounding chords. After all, one C6 or Ab7 will "work" for any other C6 or Ab7, though, obviously, C6 will not work for Ab7 or vice versa. Not all choices are shown for each chord. Be sure to swap in other positions of the same chord from other songs. Since most of the chords shown are closed-position chords, move the shapes around and identify the new chords. For example, if you move the A7 shown down one fret it becomes an Ab7. See other examples below.

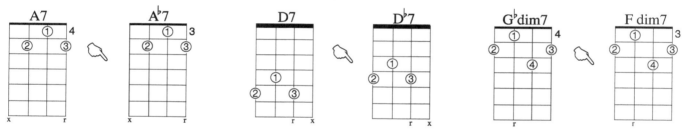

Some of the chords in this book, like the G6 on the next page, use one finger to fret two strings. If you have difficulty doing this, try alternatives that might work better for you. For example, on the first G6 use fingers one and two on strings three and two, use finger three or four on string one.

I included some chord melody passages in the melody to "Clouds and Shadows." With this technique we *arpeggiate* or play each chord tone in succession, lowest pitched note to highest, and end the arpeggio on the melody note, the highest note of the chord, giving that note more emphasis than the other chord tones. Melody notes are usually played on string one or two.

You'll find the chord melody fingerings in the chord section that follows. The circled numbers above the chord melody diagrams (① ② ③, etc.) correspond to the numbers in the music.

When you're accompanying the melody in measures one, five, seventeen, and twenty-nine, you can play the Eb7 chord on all four beats. You can also use the chord melody chord forms in your accompaniment.

When the melody is played at the head and tail of "Clouds and Shadows" the band plays "breaks" or "stops" in measures four, eight, sixteen, twenty, and twenty-eight. You could play these breaks throughout the tune during the solos, but in my humble opinion, they get a little old if they're repeated that many times.

Since acoustic stringed instruments don't have a lot of sustain, try substituting a series of quarter notes on the half and dotted half note chord melody passages. In measures twenty-three and twenty-four I play tremolo on the two tied A notes. Obviously tremolo on the mandolin can be used to increase the sustain of notes that would otherwise fade out before their full value.

Modifying Chord Forms

It's a good idea to get to know which part of a chord (1, 3, 5, 7, etc.) each note of the chord supplies. Many of the chord diagrams in this book show where the root of a form is located, if that chord includes the root. (I chose not to identify where the other tones are located, the third, fifth, seventh, etc., for clarity and simplicity.) Once you know where the root is located, you can move the chord form up and down the fingerboard to different roots. If you know where the other tones are located, you can modify them, raise or lower them and make just about any chord.

Let's look at one chord form and modify its tones one by one to make other chords. You can do the same with any chord form. We'll start with a four-note, four-string A chord. Many of the chords in this book are three-note chords and they can be modified in exactly the same way once you know what part of the chord each note supplies.

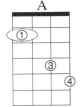

The diagram at left shows where all the chord tones are located: r = root or one, 3 = third, 5 = fifth. If there's a seventh in the chord, 7 = seventh. If the diagram includes an "x" it shows which strings/notes are not played in the form.

This form has a root or "1" of the chord in the bass and another root as the highest note of the chord. The "bass" is the lowest chord tone in this form, and it's located on the fourth string, fret two. This form can be moved up and down the fingerboard to about ten different positions to make ten different major chords, all with the root in the bass. The recipe for this form of the A major chord is 1 – 5 – 3 – 1. Other chord forms may have the third, the fifth or the seventh as the lowest note of the chord. This chord form, like all the others, gives a certain sound that's unique. It has a specific tone color and you decide when to use it, just like you'd use one color or another while painting.

If we lower or flat the third of this chord, located on string three, we'll get an Am chord with the recipe 1 – 5 – b3 – 1. This Am chord with the root in the bass is shown on the left and it too, like the A chord above, is moveable up and down the fingerboard to many different minor chords. Practice going back and forth from the A to the Am, keeping in mind that we only need to modify the third of the chord to go from one to the other.

Let's looks at a three-string G7 chord at left and modify its notes to create different chords. Again we'll need to know what part of the chord each note supplies. Since these chords only have three notes and more complex chords have four or more tones (variations of 1 – 3 – 5 – 7) we'll be leaving out one or more notes. Let's lower or flat the third, located on string four, fret four, by one half step. That changes the chord recipe to 1 – b3 – 5 – b7. In this form, the notes (lowest pitched to highest) are b3 – b7 – 5 with no root. See the diagram at right. Again this chord form can be moved up and down the fingerboard to make several minor seven chords. Therein lies the beauty of closed-position chords. Learn one form and you can use it to play about ten different chords! This movement wouldn't be possible if the chord included any open-string notes.

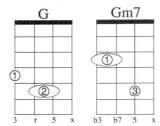

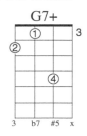

Look again at the G and Gm7 chords at left. To make the Gm7 we modified the root and third notes of the original G triad chord by lowering them. We lowered the root by one whole step to reach the flatted seventh and lowered the third by one half set to reach the flatted third. Now let's lower the fifth of the Gm7 chord. The resulting chord, a Gm7b5 ("G minor seven flat five," also known as a "half-diminished") is shown on the right.

Neither of these chord forms include the root note, in this case the G. As mentioned on page 12 we can usually omit the root without adversly affecting the sound of the chord. In an ensemble the root is often supplied by one of the other instruments. Even if the root isn't played listeners tend to "supply" it from the context of the song's chord progression. It's more important to keep the "flavor notes" of the chord. These notes, the sevenths, thirds, or any modified notes, do more to define the sound of the chord.

If we can lower or flat chord notes we can also raise or sharp them to make still more new chords. The three-string G7 chord is shown at left. If we raise the fifth of the G7 on string two (the D note) by one half step, we end up with the chord on the right, a G7+ ("G seven augmented"). We could also raise the third and seventh tones to change the chord further. You'll use the G7+ on "The World is Waiting for the Sunrise" on page 106.

Notice that the top line of the chord diagram is not as thick as it was in previous diagrams. That's because with this chord we've moved up the fingerboard a bit noted by the numeral three to the right of the diagram. This "3" tells us to place our first fretting finger in the third fret and that the top line now represents fret two and not the nut as in the previous diagrams.

This exercise demonstrates that we can make just about any chord we want by raising or lowering one or more chord tones of any three- or four-note chord form, whether it includes the root note or not. Each chord has a recipe and we alter that recipe to create new chords.

Practice modifying all the chord forms in this book. Take them one at a time, identify what part of the chord each note supplies, and experiment with raising and lowering the third, fifth, and seventh. Identify and name the resulting chord. You'll be amazed at the chords you'll discover and what you'll learn about chord theory.

Clouds and Shadows chord forms for chord-melody passages

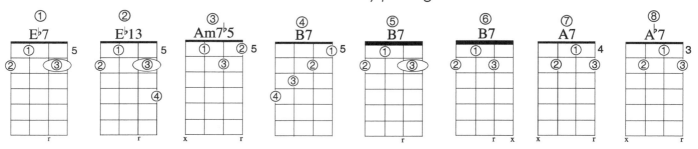

Clouds and Shadows accompaniment chords

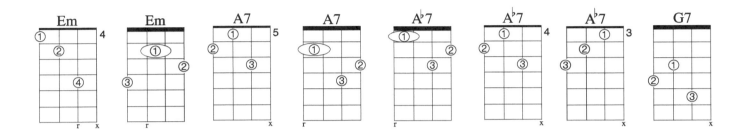

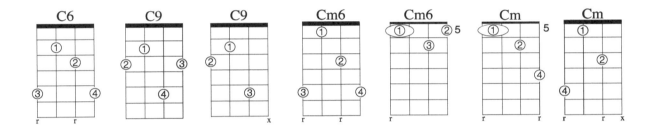

Clouds and Shadows

Key of G

Dix Bruce, 2008

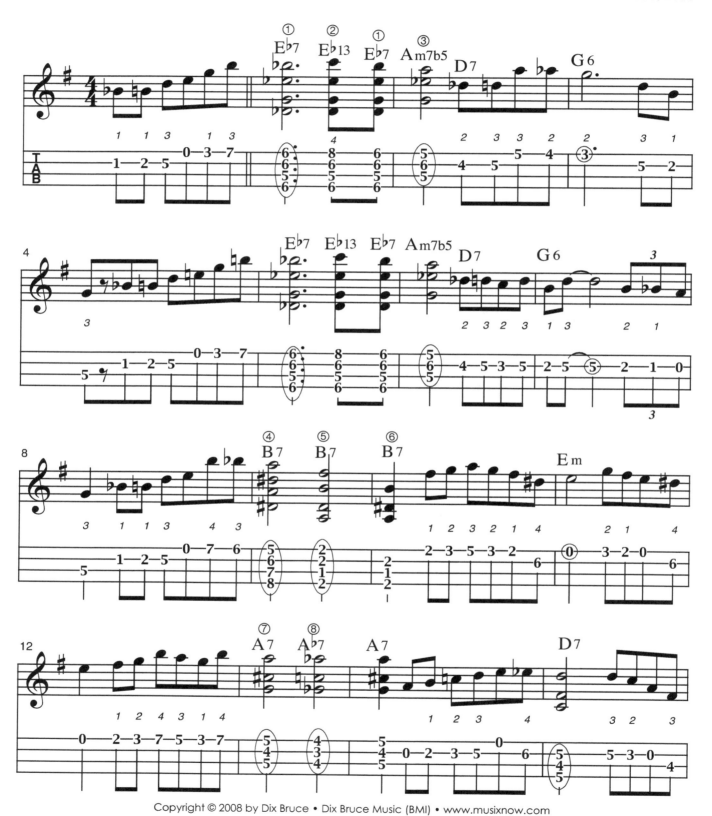

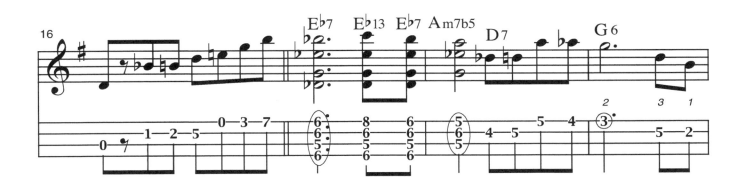

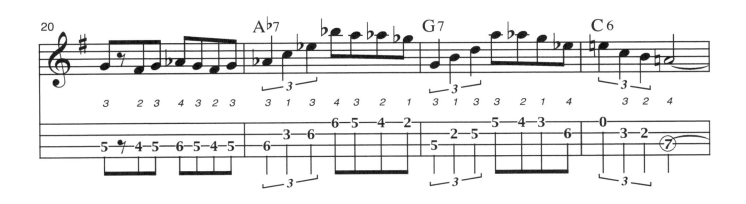

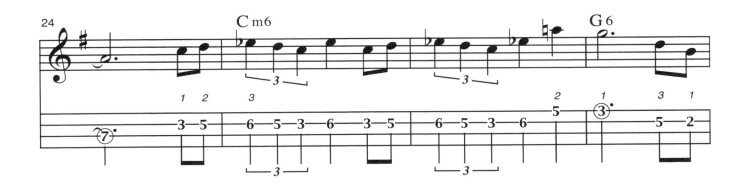

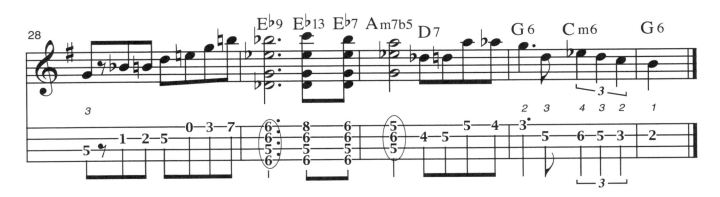

Margie

"Margie," which Django recorded several times, is one of my favorite melodies because it's so bright and perky. At the session, I added a little *rubato* guitar introduction based on a riff I heard Django play on a recording of "I'm Confessin'." I extended it and threw in some extra chords. "Rubato" means that the introduction is played out of time with the rest of the piece. The clue that the main part of the tune is about to start is the C7+ or "augmented" chord at the end of the intro. (See page 56.) It's begging to be resolved to the F, the first chord of "Margie." You can download the mandolin version of the intro chords, melody and TAB from **musixnow.com/gypsyswing2downloads/** Although the intro doesn't lay as well on the mandolin as it does on the guitar, it'll be a fun exercise to adapt and give you more experience with chord-melody playing.

When you can play "Margie" as written, try substituting F6 for the F chords. Sixth chords can often be substituted for simple I ("one") chords. Try 6s instead of the regular triad I chords on other songs in this book. For the ending on the band track we extended the final two measures to six and added a typical swing/jazz ending: iii (Am7) VI (D7) ii (Gm7) V (C7) I (F or F6). Band #1.

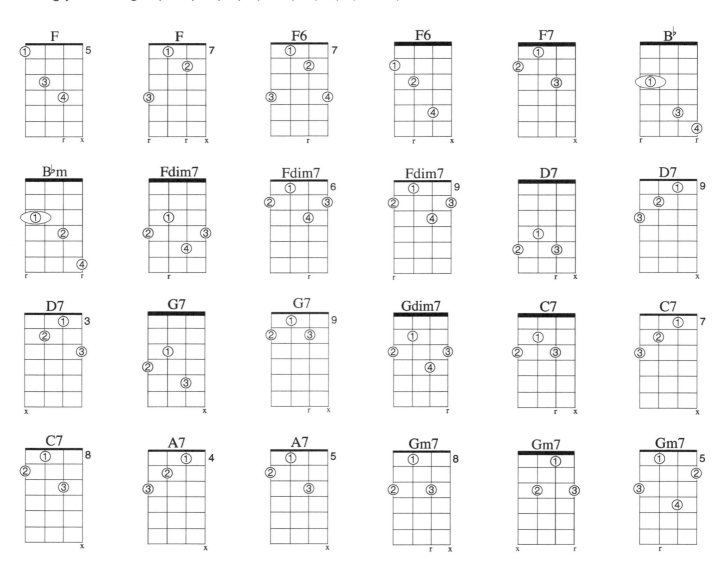

Margie

Key of F

Conrad and Robinson, 1920

Whispering

When I first started playing in jazz bands, I'd hear the other musicians talking about playing "choruses." They'd say, "I'll take two choruses, then you take one, we'll split the last chorus." I didn't have a clue what they meant, but eventually I realized that "one chorus" meant to play one solo on the chord progression. "Two choruses" meant to play twice through the chord changes. I always thought it was interesting that what I referred to as a "solo" they called a "chorus," but I didn't know exactly why until someone explained the classic pop song form to me.

When we play a song like "Oh, Lady be Good," "Avalon," or "Honeysuckle Rose," we're playing the chorus to that tune. Most often the form of the chorus is thirty-two measures in length and many follow what's called an "A–A–B–A" pattern, like "Swingin' Like '42" on page 42. The first eight measures are the first "A." The second eight are a repeat of the first eight and make up the second "A" often with a second ending or some passage that moves the song to the third eight measures or the "B." The "B" part is also referred to as the "bridge." After the "B" is played, the "A" is repeated once more. Songs like "Avalon," "Whispering" and a lot of others in this book, don't have an "A–A–B–A" form or a bridge. Instead they have some variation of a thirty-two measure form, sometimes with repeated sections.

In addition to a thirty-two measure chorus, almost all of these types of songs have a verse. The verse is rarely played in jazz and almost never soloed over. Singers do often include a verse at the beginning of a song but don't usually return to it. So, most of us have never heard the verses to the most famous songs in the world, songs we may have played hundreds of times. I thought it might be interesting to include the verse along with the chorus to "Whispering."

The verse to "Whispering" is sixteen measures in length. We play it one time only and then repeat the chorus for solos. The chorus begins with the lyric "Whispering while you cuddle near me" in measure seventeen and doesn't have an "A–A–B–A" form as mentioned above.

Don't let the sheer number of chords in "Whispering" spook you. About two-thirds of them are alternate voicings that you should eventually learn as a way of expanding your chord and position vocabulary. Take them slowly and learn a few at a time. In measure forty-five, just a few bars before the end of the chorus, the chords change on every beat from Fm7 to C7 and back. I've labelled these "optional chords" since it's tough to fit them all in. You can play the Fm7 for all four beats in this measure.

Another reason I included "Whispering" is because it's in the key of Eb. If you've come to swing and jazz through rock, country, or bluegrass music, you may be a little frightened by the key of Eb. Yes, the chords can be challenging and the melody notes are all fretted, but after a little bit of work, one key is the same as any other key. To be a versatile musician, you need to be comfortable playing in any key. I mentioned this before but think it bears repeating. Here's a likely scenario: suppose you learn "Whispering" as written in the key of Eb. You get to the gig and the singer wants you to perform it in the key of Ab. Every singer has a limited vocal range and can't change his or her voice to accommodate you. You need to accommodate the singer. If you've practiced chords and melodies in closed positions and moved both around the fingerboard, it'll be a piece of cake!

After you've played through the progression a few times, try substituting an Eb6 for the regular Eb chord. Sixth chords can often be used in this way and it's up to you to decide when and where to substitute. Though it's not written in the music, on the recording we usually play a V or Bb7 chord at the end of each chorus in measure forty-eight. The V (or dominant seven) chord sets up the return to the top of the chorus and the Eb or Eb6 chord (the "I" or "one" chord).

In measure twenty-three I added an alternate C7sus4 chord in parenthesis above the Db7. Some musicians prefer this chord to the Db7. Try both and see which you like.

When I recorded the slow melodies to most of the songs in this book, I tried to play them as written without too much variation. When I played these melodies on the up-to-speed recording or when I play in performance on the bandstand, I take liberties to make the music swing. To demonstrate this, I played around with the melody a bit on the second half of the up-to-speed "Whispering" track. I used what my good friend violinist Jeremy Cohen calls "rhythmization." To rhythmize a melody you keep the pitches the same but change the rhythm slightly and add accents. In this case I repeated a few notes and here and there added some neighboring tones. There are no set rules to rhythmization other than to stay close to the melody and vary the rhythm. Listen to the example and you'll hear what I mean. Rhythmization is a good way to dip your toe into the pool of improvisation by using the melody as your base and moving ever so slightly away from it.

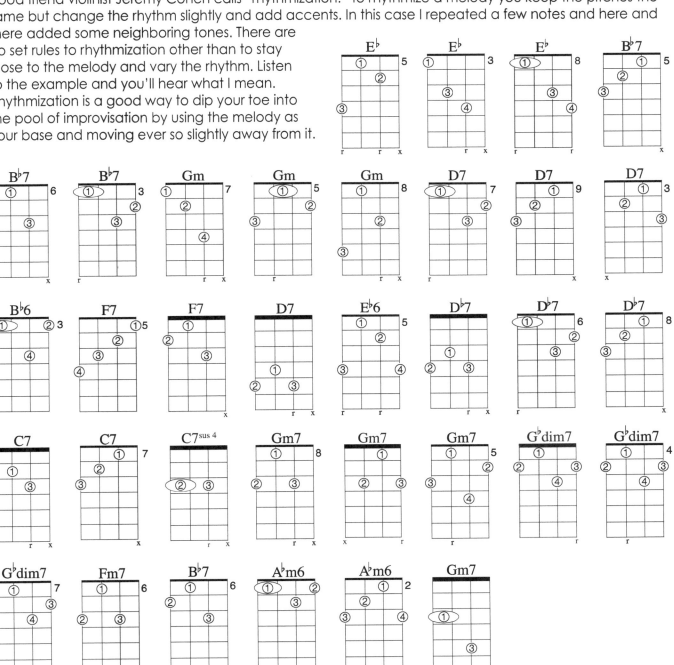

Whispering

Key of Eb

Schonberger and Schonberger, 1920

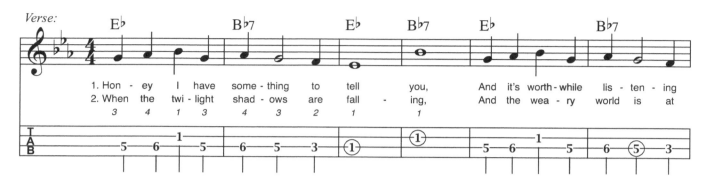

1. Hon - ey I have some - thing to tell you, And it's worth - while lis - ten - ing
2. When the twi - light shad - ows are fall - ing, And the wea - ry world is at

to._____ Put your lit - tle head on my shoul - der,
rest,_____ Then I'll whis - per just why I know dear,

So that I can whis - per to you. Whis - per - ing while you cud - dle
Lov - ing time is al - ways the best.

near me, Whis - per - ing so no one can hear me,

Arrangement © 2008 by Dix Bruce • Dix Bruce Music (BMI) • www.musixnow.com

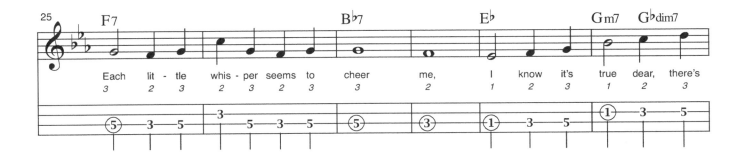

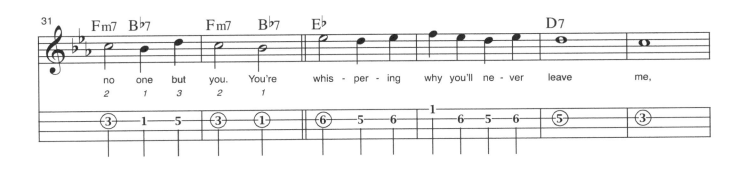

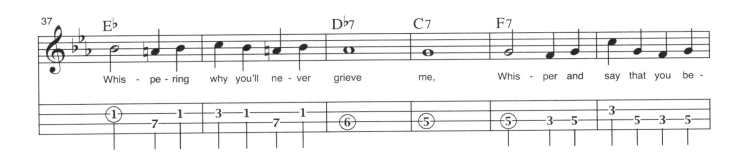

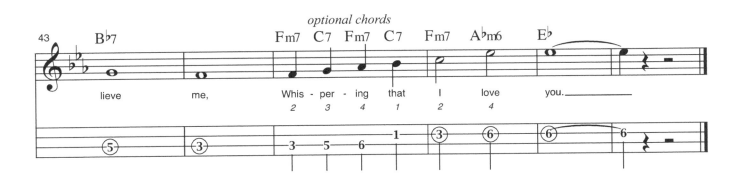

El Choclo

"El Choclo" is a tango. The rhythmic structure is "ONE–two–three–four–AND, ONE–two–three–four–AND," with accents on beat one and the "and" after the fourth beat. Sort of: "ONE–two–three–four–AHH, CHOO–two–three–four–AHH." This is quite different from the typical swing rhythm of "cha–chuk, cha–chuk." The band plays "breaks" on the A7 chord at measure twenty-seven in each chorus. Jason Vanderford continues to play a light rhythm in the space to keep us all in time. When you're soloing, you can either leave this space empty or play through it. I use tremolo on the two tied A notes of the melody in measures twenty-six and twenty-seven to increase their sustain and tension.

"El Choclo" is in two different — though related — keys: Dm ("D minor") and F major. It modulates from Dm to F major after the first sixteen measures. It doesn't stay in F major for long, only four measures, and then the A7 in measure twenty-one, the dominant seven chord of Dm, brings it back to Dm. Just enough to give the progression a nice change of pace and texture. The keys of Dm and F major are keys that are relative to one another and share the same key signature. The key of Dm is the "relative minor" of the key of F, built on the sixth note of the F major scale. The key of F can also be said to be the "relative major" of Dm. That's why the key signature doesn't change.

When you solo on "El Choclo" you'll use the D harmonic minor scale where the seventh tone, the C, is raised to C# to allow us to make the A7 chord: A – C# – E – G. (See page 28.)

At the very end of the song we added a strong and fairly typical ending, i – V – i ("one – five – one") to finalize and tie things up. It leaves no doubt that we're finished with the song. Reminder: when we refer to chords in a key, we use uppercase Roman numerals (I, VI, II, V) for majors and dominants, lower case (i, iii, vi, etc.) for minors and diminished chords.

I left several open-string notes in the tablature to "El Choclo" to make it somewhat easier to play. When you've memorized the melody as written, try substituting fretted notes for the open ones to discover a closed-position, moveable version of the melody.

You'll notice that I included several different chord diagrams for the Ab diminished seven chord (Abdim7 or Ab°7). These are all the same chord form but played at different frets. How can the same Abdim7 chord form be played at different frets and still be an Abdim7 ?

Well, the diminished seven chord behaves differently than any other chord. The recipe for a diminished seven, also known as a *fully diminished* chord, is 1 – b3 – b5 – bb7 or "one – flat three – flat five – doubly flatted seven." If we take a C chord, C – E – G, and add a flatted seventh tone to it, a Bb, we'll get a C7 chord, a dominant seven chord, with the notes C – E – G – Bb. (The recipe for any dominant seven chord like C7 is 1 – 3 – 5 – b7.) To turn that C7 into a Cdim7 we'll need to flat the third, flat the fifth, and flat again the already flattened b7 like this: C – Eb – Gb – Bbb.

The intervals between the notes of a diminished seven chord are all minor thirds or three half steps. A minor third interval on the mandolin fingerboard is three frets. That means that if we move any diminished seven chord three frets up or down the fingerboard from its original position, it'll still be the same chord, just a different inversion. That's why we can play the Abdim7 at the third fret, move it up to the sixth fret, and then up to the ninth fret and we'll have Abdim7. If you can reach it on your mandolin this same form at the twelfth fret will also be Abdim7.

Another unique thing about diminished chords is that any note in the chord can name it. So, the Cdim7 chord is also Ebdim7, Gbdim7, and Bbbdim7. OK, I agree with you, most people think of Bbb as an A note but theoretically speaking it's a Bbb note here and not an A. That's because the recipe for the diminished seven chord is 1 – b3 – b5 – bb7 not 1 – b3 – b5 – 6. The A would be the sixth tone of the chord. I know it might seem like a silly point, but when we're discussing such things we want to keep our thinking as ordered as possible. Chords are defined as notes with intervals of thirds between them. We find thirds, major or minor thirds, between a one and a three, a two and a four, a three and a five, where three numbers (1, 2, 3; 2, 3, 4, etc.) are spanned, but not between a five and a six where only two numbers are spanned. The upshot is that there are only three different diminished seven chords, but we can name them in different ways to make any diminished seven chord we need.

Try all the different diminished seven chords shown below in "El Choclo" and also on all the other songs in this book with diminished seven chords. Move the different forms around the fingerboard and identify the different names of each. If you do that you'll eventually know several positions for any diminished seven chord! See page 88 for info on playing over diminished seven chords.

"El Choclo" became a pop hit with English lyrics in the early 1950s as "Kiss of Fire." It was recorded by Georgia Gibbs, Tony Martin, Louis Armstrong, Guy Lombardo, and Billy Eckstine, among others. Of course Homer and Jethro's major key version of "Lil' Ol' Kiss of Fire" is hilarious.

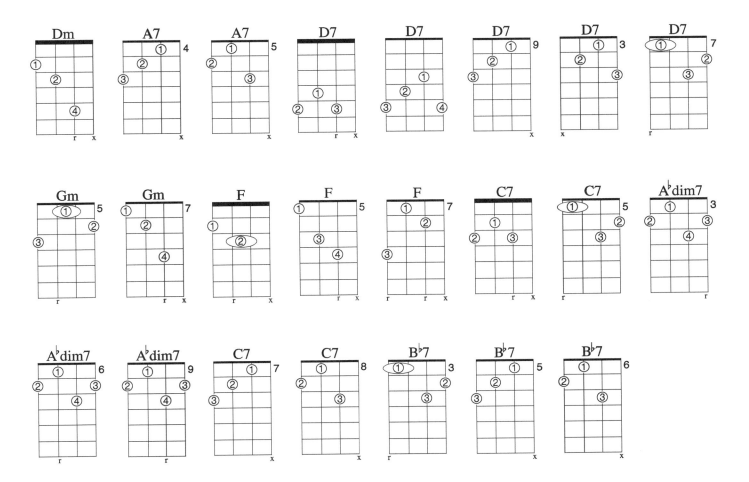

El Choclo

Key of Dm

Angel G. Villoldo, 1903

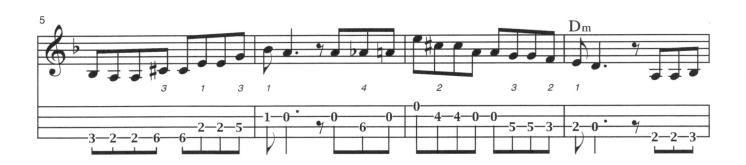

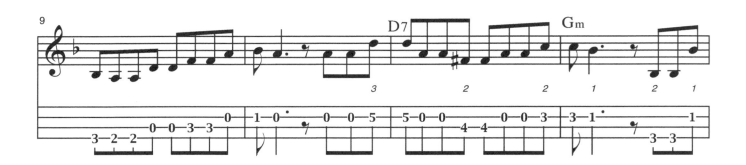

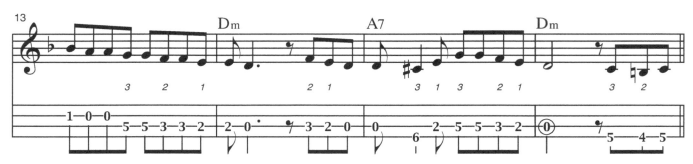

(Back Home Again in)
Indiana

"*(Back Home Again in)* Indiana" is another "must know" standard. Historically jazz musicians of all stripes have worked on its changes endlessly, and you should too. Our arrangement is in two keys, F and Ab. The modulation from F to Ab takes the song up an interval of a minor third, or three half-steps. Many standards like "China Boy" (page 35) and "Swingin' Like 42" (page 42) use a minor or major third modulation within a chorus to change the key of the middle eight bars or "bridge." We'll change keys on the entire chorus of "Indiana." After you play it twice in the key of F, you'll play an Eb7 chord, which might seem like an odd chord in the key of F. It *is* odd, mainly because the Eb7 is *not* in the key of F. However, the Eb7 is the V or dominant seven chord of the key of Ab, our new key. Using the V of the key we're approaching is a typical way to modulate in pop and jazz music, and we'll use the same method on "Django's Djazz Blues" (page 74) to move the tune through seven keys. We'll play "Indiana" twice through in Ab and then modulate back to the key of F, again using the V or dominant seven chord of the new key, C7, to bring us back to the key of F for one more ride through the changes.

I've placed the melodies in two different regions of the fingerboard. Learning both of these closed-position melodies will allow you to play "Indiana" in two octaves in several keys.

We talked about chord numbering on page 42. Let's explore the subject a little further. Note and chord numbers are relative to a section or song's home key. In the first full measure of "Indiana" the chords walk down from F to D7. (Ignore the passing E7 and Eb7 chords for now.) What chord numbers should we assign to this progression? A lot of musicians would describe this as "one – six." Would that be right? Let's diagram the F major scale.

Scale:	F	G	A	Bb	C	D	E	F
Interval:		w	w	h	w	w	w	h
Note #:	1	2	3	4	5	6	7	8 or 1
Chord #:	I	ii	iii	IV	V	vi	vii°	VIII or I
Chords:	F	Gm	Am	Bb	C	Dm	Edim	F

According to the diagram the six chord in the key of F is Dm, not D7. Could we still call the D7 a six? As mentioned above, lots of musicians do. However, if we use the term "six chord" in this way how will musicians know if the chord should be Dm or D7? Dm and D7 are very different chords, and different chords have different functions within a key.

We've discussed how a V or dominant seven chord pulls our ear toward its I ("one") chord. Likewise ii, iii, IV, vi, and vii° chords all have unique functions, and we confuse them at our peril. A more precise and theoretically correct way to describe this progression is to look at the function of each chord. It's clear that F is the I chord. The D7 is a dominant, and that means it's pulling us toward a I. D is the V of G so the D7 is pulling our ear to G or G minor. And how does G relate to our home key of F? It's a two. So D7 in this case is best described, at least functionally, as "the five of two." When we get to the expected G it's a G7, another dominant that leads to a C. The G7 here is best described functionally as the "five of five" since C is the five of our original key of F. Again, the G7 leads to C but when we reach the C, it's dominant: C7. C7 leads to the F so the C7 is truly a V. The whole progression, F – D7 – G7 – C7 – F can be described as "one – five of two – five of five – five – one." This is not to say that musicians who call this progression "one – six – two – five – one" are wrong. It just may not tell the whole story. And, admittedly, that's a mouthful to say on the bandstand. An alternate way to describe this progression that might be more to the point is to simply call it a "cycle of fifths" progression or to describe the D7 and G7 chords as "six dominant" and "two dominant. Whatever is understood and works on the bandstand is right!

(Back Home Again in) Indiana accompaniment chords, key of F

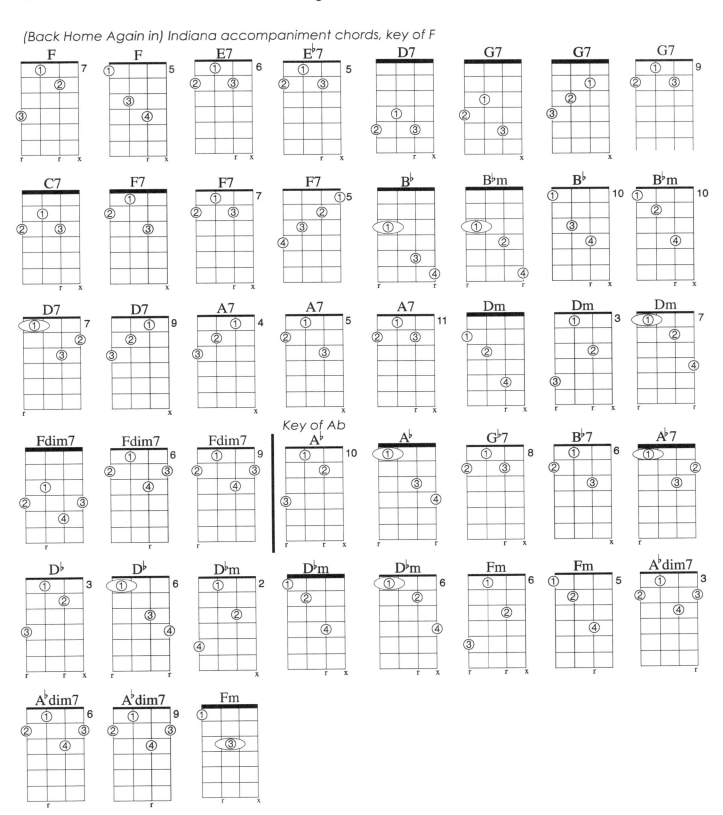

(Back Home Again in)
Indiana

Keys of F and Ab

Hanley and MacDonald, 1917

Django's Djazz Blues

Transposing from one key to another, as we did with "Indiana," can be difficult and confusing at first. The chart below shows the major scales for all the keys, their key signatures and the chords in each key. The chart can be used as a transposition guide. The chords are *triads* (three-note chords) and all made using *only* the notes of the associated major scale. More complex chords like dominant sevens and fully diminished sevens require additional notes, some "borrowed" from other scales/keys. Scales are listed horizontally with Arabic numerals, 1-8/1, chords with Roman numerals, I-VIII/I. To read a scale simply ignore the chord markings ("m" for minor or "°" for diminished). To determine chords, read horizontally.

Scale, Chord, and Transposition Chart

Key	#/b	Scale / Chord	1 (do) / I	2 (re) / ii	3 (me) / iii	4 (fa) / IV	5 (so) / V	6 (la) / vi	7 (ti) / vii°	8 (do) / VIII
C	none		C	Dm	Em	F	G	Am	B°	C
F	1-b		F	Gm	Am	Bb	C	Dm	E°	F
Bb	2-b		Bb	Cm	Dm	Eb	F	Gm	A°	Bb
Eb	3-b		Eb	Fm	Gm	Ab	Bb	Cm	D°	Eb
Ab	4-b		Ab	Bbm	Cm	Db	Eb	Fm	G°	Ab
Db	5-b		Db	Ebm	Fm	Gb	Ab	Bbm	C°	Db
Gb	6-b		Gb	Abm	Bbm	Cb	Db	Ebm	F°	Gb
Cb	7-b		Cb	Dbm	Ebm	Fb	Gb	Abm	Bb°	Cb
C#	7-#		C#	D#m	E#m	F#	G#	A#m	B#°	C#
F#	6-#		F#	G#m	A#m	B	C#	D#m	E#°	F#
B	5-#		B	C#m	D#m	E	F#	G#m	A#°	B
E	4-#		E	F#m	G#m	A	B	C#m	D#°	E
A	3-#		A	Bm	C#m	D	E	F#m	G#°	A
D	2-#		D	Em	F#m	G	A	Bm	C#°	D
G	1-#		G	Am	Bm	C	D	Em	F#°	G

For example, the major scale for the key of Bb (2 flats) is:

Bb	C	D	Eb	F	G	A	Bb
1	2	3	4	5	6	7	8 or 1
do	re	me	fa	so	la	ti	do

The chords for the same key are:

Bb	Cm	Dm	Eb	F	Gm	A°	Bb
I	ii	iii	IV	V	vi	vii°	VII or I

This chart can help you transpose melodies and chords from one key to another. Here's how: Let's say you know a tune in the key of D but want to be able to play it in the key of G and don't know what chords to play. The key of D chords, which you already know, are D, G, and A. From the key of D line of the chart you can see that the D is the I chord, the G is the IV, and the A is the V. To transpose these chords to the key of G, just follow down in their respective columns (I, ii, iii, etc.) to the new key of G. This will tell you to substitute Gs for all the D (I) chords, Cs for all the G (IV) chords, and Ds for all the A (V)chords. Like chords are always substituted, I to I, ii to ii, vii° to vii°, etc.

You can also transpose note by note using the chart. Continuing with the above example, let's say the first note of the tune in the key of D is an F# and you need to know what the first note in the key of G will be. Find the key of D line in the chart, read over horizontally until you come to the F#, which happens to be in the "3" column. Stay in the "3" column and follow down to the key of G line, presto, you see that the first note of our tune in the new key of G is B.

"Django's Djazz Blues" is a simple riff blues I put together as an exercise in playing blues chord changes and leads in several different keys. It begins in the key of G, then modulates to C, F, Bb, Eb, Ab, and Db. The movement is by intervals of perfect fourths. C is a perfect fourth "above" G, F is a perfect fourth "above" C, and so on. We'll play the changes twice through in each key. At the end of the second time through each chord progression we'll change the one chord to a dominant seven (G to G7, C to C7, F to F7, etc.) to facilitate the modulation. Once we make the chord into a dominant seven, it becomes the V ("five chord") of the key we're moving into and pulls our ear to the new key.

You'll find the first two keys printed on the following page. You should be able to move the closed-position chords and melody to the other keys. If you have trouble, you can download the complete music in all keys with melodies, tablature, and chords from **musixnow.com/gypsyswing2downloads**. Be sure to give it a good solid try on your own first, as you'll learn much more by working through the process.

Notice that fret-wise the positions of the notes in the key of C version are identical to those of the key of G, just moved over by one string on the fingerboard. The melody spans three strings. If your first note is located on string one, you can move the whole melody "over" one string and you'll transpose it "up" an interval of a fourth though the sound will be lower in pitch. Ab to Db, A to D, Bb to Eb, B to F#, C to F, and so on. Look for similar visual clues and relationships as you move through the keys of the arrangement.

All of the individual closed-position chords shown below can be moved up and down the fingerboard to make the new chords in the new keys. Try moving whole sets of chords from one key to the new keys. For example, you can move the C set to Eb by moving each chord up three frets.

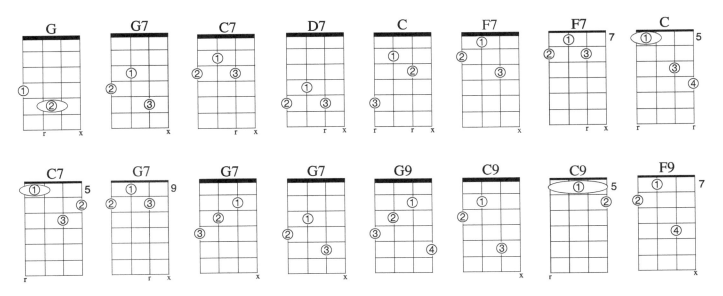

Django's Djazz Blues

Keys of G, C, F, Bb, Eb, Ab, Db

Dix Bruce, 2008

Red Wing Swing

"Red Wing Swing" is based on the old pop song "Red Wing." Django Reinhardt and Stephane Grappelli arranged and recorded several old pop and ethnic songs in the Hot Club style. This version of "Red Wing" was inspired by their recording of "Swanee River." They tear it up, as the song modulates to different keys like "Django's Djazz Blues" on page 74.

To make "Red Wing" swing we first added a Hot Club rhythm section to it. To come up with a swingy melody, I played through the straight melody several times until I gradually rhythmized it in a way that stayed in my head. Try turning your own favorite old songs into Swing and Gypsy Swing vehicles.

Once you're comfortable with the chord progression as written, try substituting in a C6 wherever you see a C chord. If you can't find the specific 6 chord that you need below, move one of the given 6 chords to the proper position on the fingerboard. Since all the chords in this book are in closed positions, they're all moveable. The C6 forms shown below can be moved up the fingerboard (toward the bridge, up in pitch) to C#6, D6, D#6, E6, F6, and so on to as many positions as you can reach. The same chords can be moved down the fingerboard (toward the nut, down in pitch).

Experiment with adding in a C7 wherever the progression moves from a C to an F chord or from a I to a IV. A C7 chord on the two or four beats before the F pulls the ear toward the new chord. Try adding the C7 in measures 2, 10, the last two beats of 16, and measure 24. See if you like the effect. Look through the other songs in this book and identify similar passages in all keys and try adding in the I7 chord before the IV.

The melody to "Red Wing Swing" is shown in the lower octave with some open-string notes. Try moving these open-string notes, except the fourth string open G, to fretted notes. Also try moving the melody up an octave to a closed position and then to other keys up and down and across the fingerboard. You can download a copy of the upper octave version from my web site: **musixnow.com/gypsyswing2downloads/** Be sure to try it on your own first. After you have moved and transposed a few melodies successfully the process will become routine.

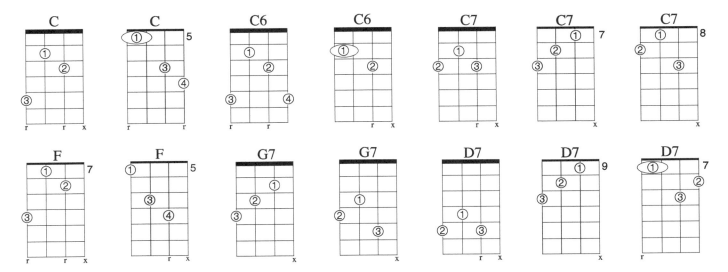

Red Wing Swing

Key of C

Mills and Chattaway, 1907; Dix Bruce, 2008

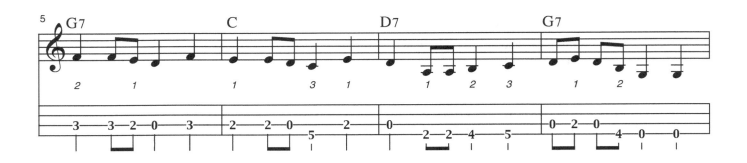

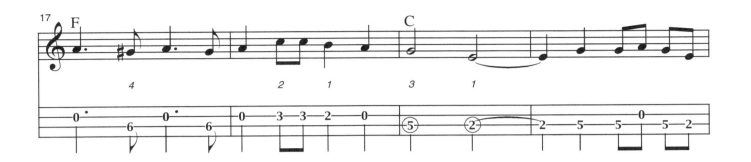

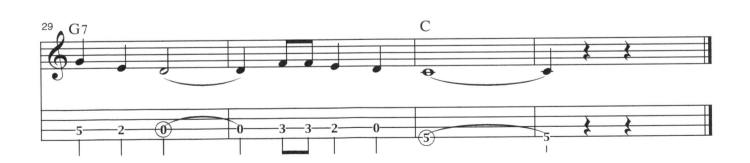

Original sheet music covers to, top: "Red Wing" (page 77), and right, "Stumbling" (page 81).

Stumbling

The melody to "Stumbling" is built around a repeating five-note phrase of four eighth notes and a quarter note. The phrase ends on a different accented beat each time: first on beat three of measure one, then beat two of measure two, then beat one of measure three, where the melody changes to half notes. It gives the song a very unsettled rhythmic feel, which is of course what makes it so interesting.

I've added some chord melody passages in measures three, four, nineteen, and twenty. They add a nice dimension to the single-string melody. We did something similar on "Clouds and Shadows" (page 54). To play them, hold the chord shown and *arpeggiate* it (play the chord's notes in succession) from the lowest pitched note to the highest. The melody note will be on string one. Try adding in octaves on the half notes in measures three, four, nineteen, and twenty. Give it a try!

When you can comfortably play the melody from memory, try playing all the open-string notes as fretted notes like in the last line. Next, try moving the melody down an octave. The regular speed recording includes the lower octave melody. Also try moving the F melody up two frets to the key of G or down two frets to Eb. You can download the lower octave version of the music and MP3 from my website. **musixnow.com/gypsyswing2downloads/**

Chord melody chords

Accompaniment chords

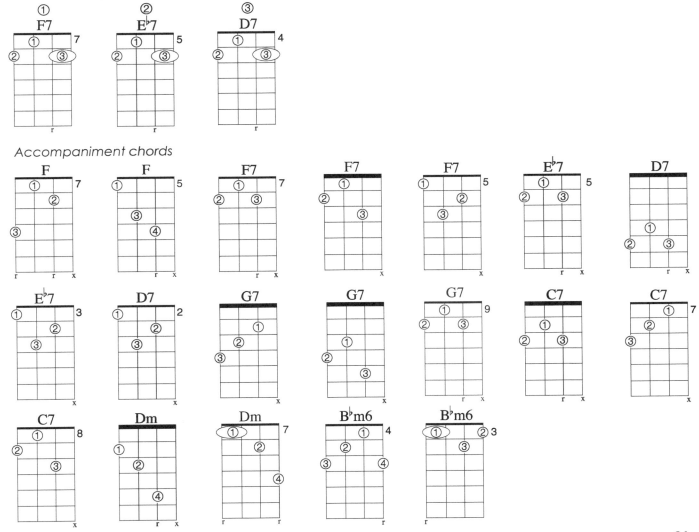

Stumbling

Key of F

Z. Confrey, 1922

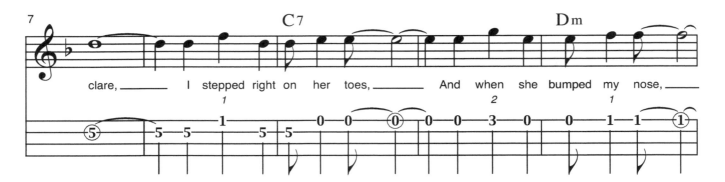

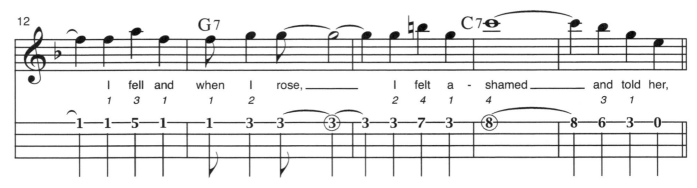

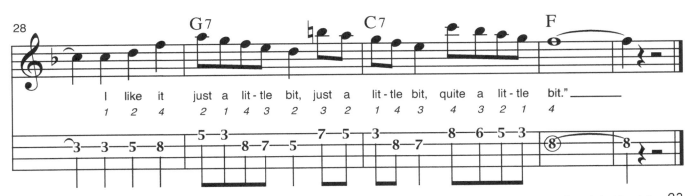

Tiger Rag

"Tiger Rag" is probably the most challenging song in this book. But once you understand the road map and real estate of it, you'll find it to be a delight. "Tiger Rag" is one of the first and most famous "jass" tunes to enjoy wide-spread popularity. It was written and recorded by The Original Dixieland Jazz Band in 1917 before the term "jass" became "jazz." Django and Stephane recorded "Tiger Rag" several times. My favorite is their duet version from 1934. Incredible! You can download a transcription of the first part of their duet from my website. Our version is played at a more moderate tempo. (Django and Stephane also recorded a completely different tune called "Django's Tiger" in 1946.)

"Tiger Rag" has three modulations or key changes that lead the tune through four different keys. The first part, marked in the music with a boxed A, is in the key of Bb. It's played twice. After that, it modulates to F, marked with a boxed B. Part B includes several rhythmic hits and accents. In measure 17 you'll see the direction "D.S. al coda." That means to go back to the 𝄋 sign at the beginning of the tune, play this part again, until you come to the "to coda" in measure 7. From here you'll skip down to measure 18 where you see the coda sign: 𝄌. This leads you to part C, which is in the key of Eb, noted with a boxed C. We're only at the bottom of the first page and we've already played in Bb, F, Bb, and now Eb!

After measure 43 you'll find one more modulation, this time to the key of Ab, marked with a boxed D at measure 43. Parts A, B, and C are played only at the beginning of the tune. Both parts C and D include accented rhythmic stops for the whole band. (See measures 21 & 22, 25 & 26, 33 & 34, 57 & 58.) These leave spaces that are often filled by another soloist or whoever is not playing the melody at that point. You can leave these spaces open but it's usually a good idea to fill them with your fantastic riffs. They'll be in the spotlight as the band drops out and all attention is on you. Solos are played over part D in the key of Ab.

The lyric "Hold that tiger" is often sung over part D. If the tune is played instrumentally by a traditional jazz band, the trombone or tuba usually mimics a tiger's roar after each melodic phrase. In that spirit, I added lots of loose slides to the performance of the melody in part D.

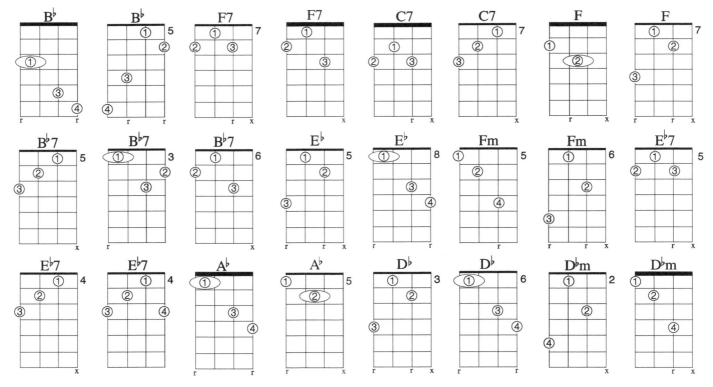

Tiger Rag

Keys of Bb, F, Eb, and Ab

Original Dixieland Jazz Band, 1917

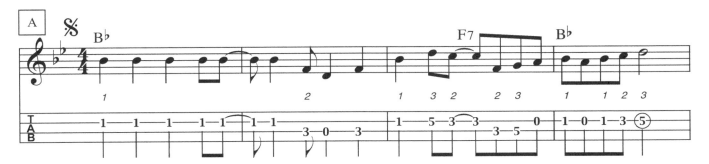

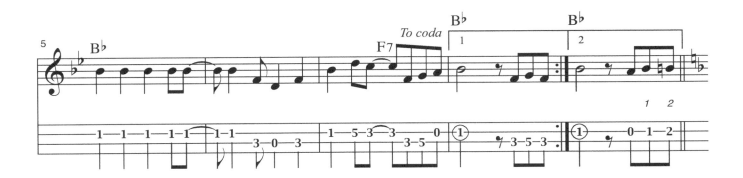

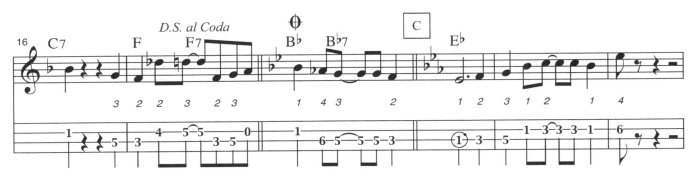

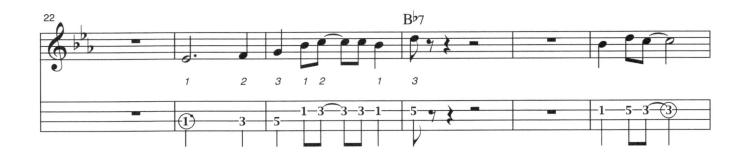

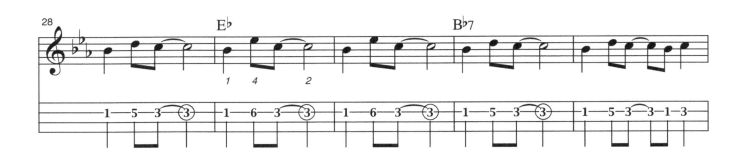

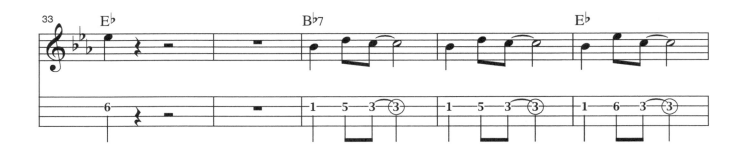

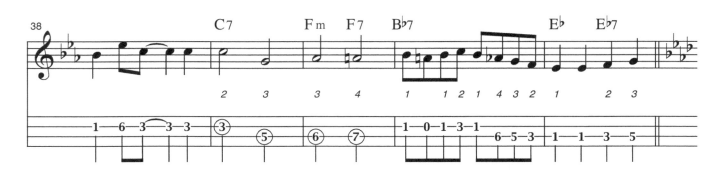

The Mysterious Diminished Seven Chord

One of the most mysterious chords is the diminished seven. It has truly unique and magic qualities. (You can read more about it on page 66.) Diminished seven chords can be difficult to solo over. It helped me to visualize where all the notes of a diminished seven chord were located on the fingerboard. These note positions formed a pattern that gave me a visual starting point.

The first two diagrams below show the chord tones of the A diminished seven chord starting with the third finger root on the fifth fret of string one. Roots, in this case A notes, are shown with a circled "R." Any of the notes of a diminished seven can be considered a "root" and name the chord. The diagram on the upper left below shows positions, fingerings, and the parts of the A°7 that each note/position supplies. The diagram on the right is the same except that I removed the fingering and chord information so that you could see the pattern of the notes more clearly. Play the A°7 descending arpeggio starting with your third finger on string one, fret five, and continuing through string four, fret two. Now play the same thing ascending. Gradually you'll see the pattern emerge.

This pattern is moveable up and down the fingerboard and can be used to map the tones of any diminished seven chord. The bottom two diagrams show the Ab°7/G#°7 notes and the Bb°7/A#°7 notes. These three different diagrams map the notes to every diminished seven chord. As you read on page 66, there are really only three different diminished seven chords. You can also find diminished seven chord notes at other positions on the fingerboard, above and below those shown. This pattern is meant to get you started.

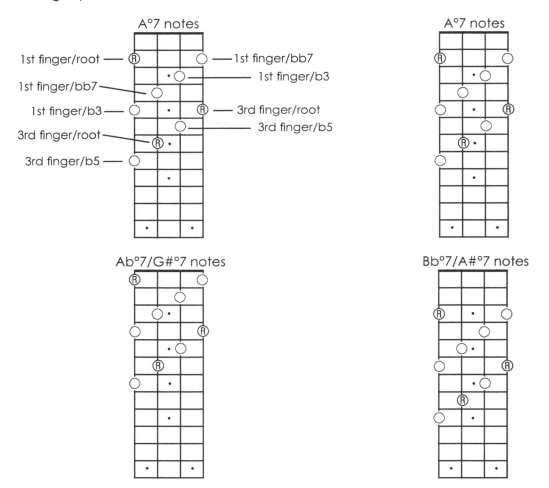

21st Century Blues

The melody to "21st Century Blues" is structured like a riff blues, a bit like "Django's Jazz Blues" on page 74, except that this has a longer form and has rhythm breaks in the second part.

We've talked about blue notes before. Generally speaking they are the flatted third and flatted seventh notes of the major scale. In the case of the key of G, those notes are the Bb and F natural notes and both are used quite a bit in the melody. Try including them in your improvisations.

The blue notes in this melody can be easily found by looking for the accidentals in the standard notation. By "accidentals" I mean the flat (♭) and natural (♮) signs that tell you to modify a scale note. An accidental doesn't always indicate a blue note, but they're a good indication in a lot of melodies.

The chord progression has a slightly unusual chord in measures ten and twenty-three, an Eb7. We've seen it before in "Clouds and Shadows" on page 54, and we'll see it again in "Way Down Yonder in New Orleans" on page 101. I think of this as simply raising the usual dominant chord in the key of G, the D7, up by one half step to add a little interest and tension. Try including the notes of the Eb7 chord at that point in your improvisations.

On the up-to-speed recordings of most of the remaining songs in this book you can hear more examples of me rhythmizing the melody to make it swing more. Compare this to the slow versions of the melodies, which are played more as written. Once again the idea is to keep the pitches pretty much the same, but to vary the rhythm with syncopation, doubling up notes, and changing rhythms. It's a good way to easily improvise on a melody and make it into a solo.

The recordings of "21st Century Blues" and the songs that follow feature two different bands. The personnel of each is listed on page 7. "21st Century Blues" is played by Band #2.

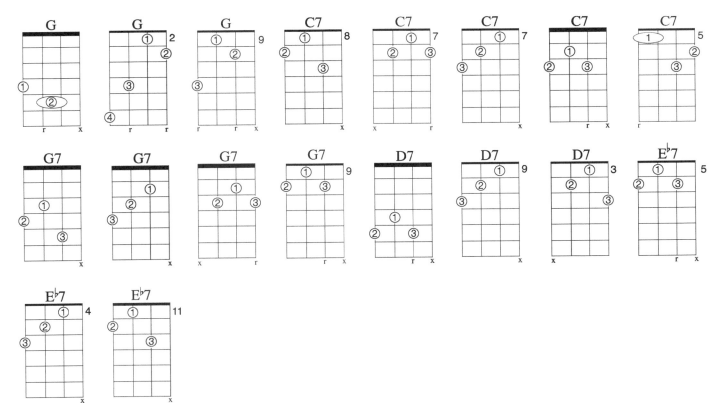

21st Century Blues

Key of G

by Dix Bruce

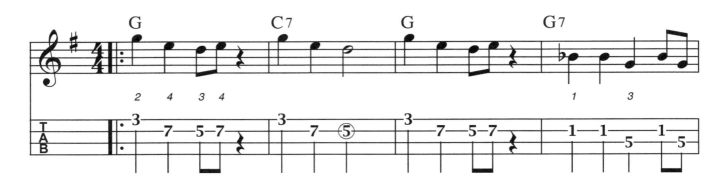

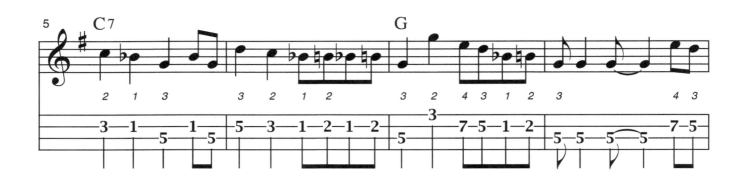

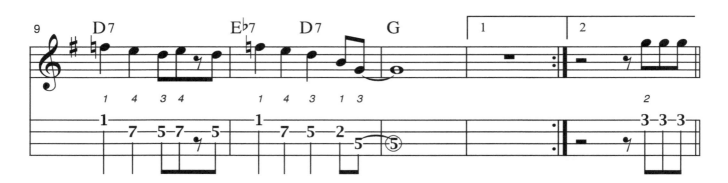

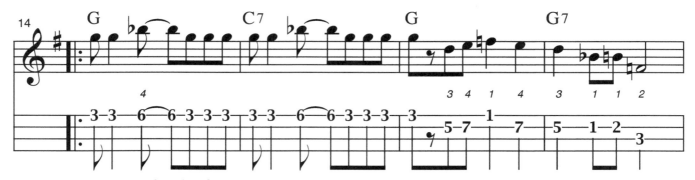

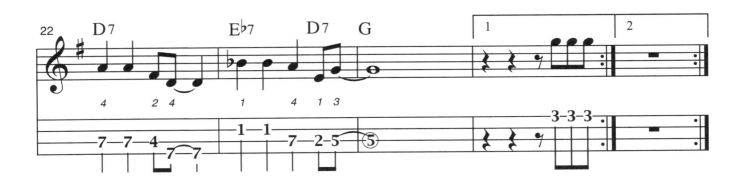

Stephane Grappelli
1750 Arch Street Studios, Berkeley, CA, ca. 1982.
Recording with David Grisman for Grisman's "Dawg Jazz/Dawg Grass" recording.

The Japanese Sandman

"The Japanese Sandman" is a straightforward and sweet old pop tune that begins and ends in the key of F. Notice how it modulates to the key of A, up a major third, in measure eleven, similar to "China Boy" (page 35) and "Swingin' Like '42 (page 42) where the bridge (or middle eight measures) modulates up a minor third. Previously we discussed how the dominant seven chord of a destination key can be used to pull a section of a song to that new key. But here there's no transition chord in measure ten moving the song from the key of F to the key of A. Try adding one. The dominant seven chord in the key of A is E7, so try playing an E7 on beat four of measure ten and see if you like the effect.

There's also no key signature change from one flat, key of F, to three sharps, key of A, before measure eleven. Instead we added sharp and natural signs to the individual melody notes and that has the same effect as a key signature change. Either way will work. I chose this method since the passage in the key of A is so short.

Once again, the collections of chords shown for each song are expanding. Don't be intimidated by their sheer numbers. Explore them a few at a time and try to choose groups of chords by their position on the fingerboard. As you move from chord to chord, avoid jumps of more than two or three frets and choose chords accordingly. Of course you may decide that you like the sound of chords that are far apart and that's fine. Go for efficiency first and play as many of a progression's chords as physically close to one another as possible.

I suggest using the fourth fretting finger in measures, six, twelve, thirteen, eighteen, twenty-three, and thirty of the melody to avoid playing open-string notes. You could play these notes unfretted and on open strings. Of course by doing that you'll lose the ability to easily move this melody to other keys up the fingerboard.

You'll get a good long two-measure ride on a diminished seven chord, the Fdim7, in measures twenty-seven and twenty-eight. Review pages 66 and 88 for more info on the diminished seven chord and what notes you can play over it. Chord tones and melody notes are always appropriate. There's also an F#dim7 in measure fifteen, but only for two beats.

On the band track I added several ascending and descending guitar bass runs that lead to the root of chords. I did it to add a little variation to the rhythm section. Again, as with rhythmizing, I just played what I was feeling at the time. I did consciously try to have the runs, from two or three frets below or above the root, fit rhythmically with the rest of the band and to not be too prominent or compete with whatever the lead player might want to do. Played by Band #1.

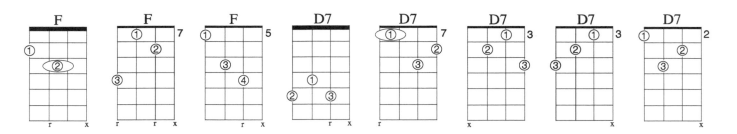

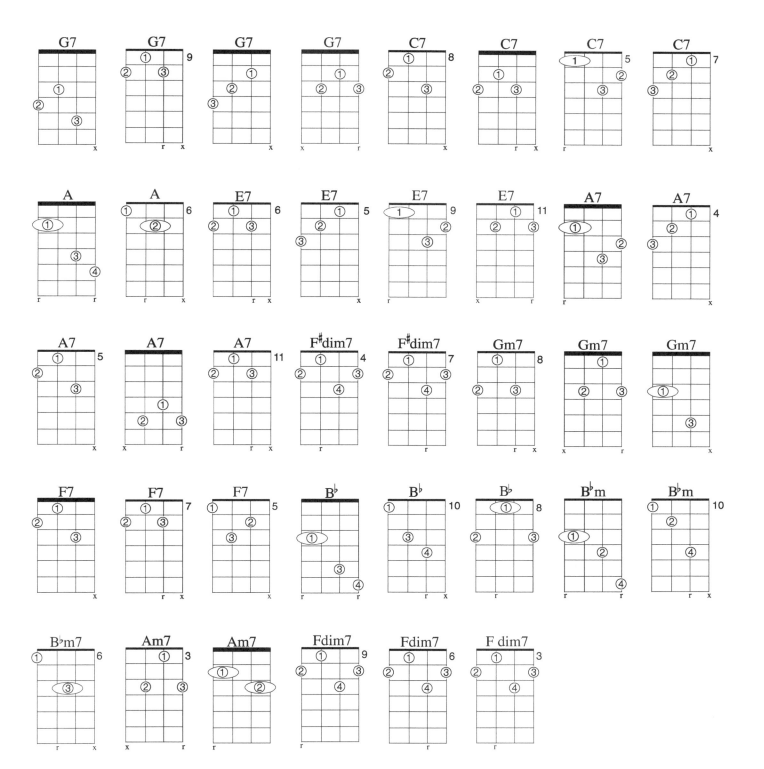

The Japanese Sandman

Key of F

Whiting and Egan, 1920

Here's the Jap-an-ese Sand - man, ___ Sneak-ing on with the dew, ___ Just an old sec-ond hand man, ___ He'll buy your old day from you. He will take ev - ery sor - row, ___ Of the day that is through, ___ And he'll give you to - mor - row, ___ Just to start life a - new. ___ Then you'll be a bit

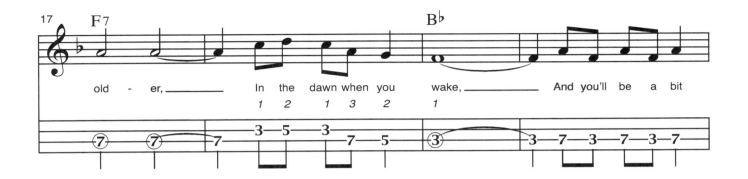

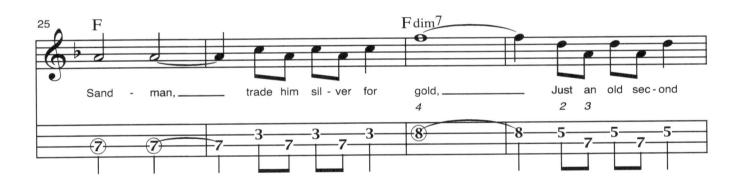

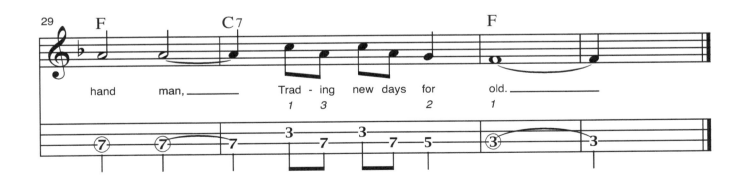

My Melancholy Baby

"My Melancholy Baby" was recorded again and again over the early years of the twentieth century and was a huge hit for several different artists. I've read that the first entertainer to sing it publicly was William Frawley, Fred Mertz from "I Love Lucy." He may have sung it on that show and I may have heard it there first. (I kept telling my mother how educational TV was!) "My Melancholy Baby" is a nice song that unfortunately got type-cast into a cliché.

The cliché is that drunks always pester the singer and the band to perform the song with a slurred and shouted "Sing *Melancholy Baby!*" This charming custom may have originated in the 1954 Judy Garland version of "A Star is Born" wherein a drunk continually shouts "Sing *Melancholy Baby!*" until the band gives up and the song is performed.

Sometimes life imitates art, and I've had the pleasure of hearing drunks shout it out at all kinds of musical events high and low – in bars, night clubs, theatres, and wedding venues. It usually gets a laugh, at least from the drunk's pals, but all this notoriety has turned a perfectly good song into a punch line. It's my mission to revive the song for its own sake, and with your help we can restore it to its former glory. We played it up-tempo on the recording but it also makes a beautiful ballad. Be sure to play this one at your upcoming gigs!

Try moving the diminished seven chords to other positions up and down the fingerboard as discussed on page 88.

Lots of rhythmizing and doubling notes on the up-to-speed melody recording. Compare it to the slow version with its more regular and straight rhythm. Played by Band #1.

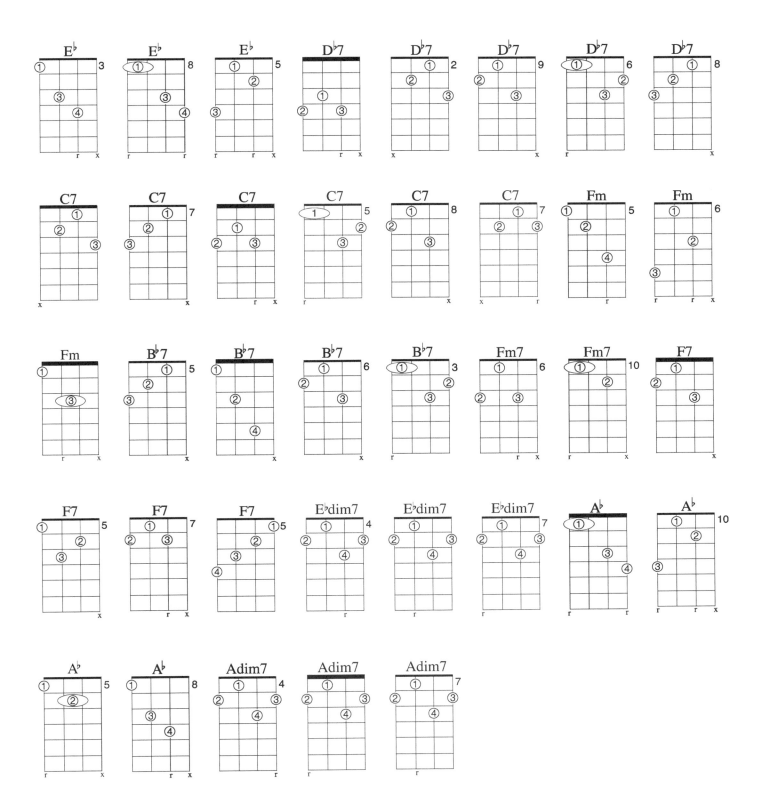

My Melancholy Baby

Key of Eb

E. Burnett, 1912

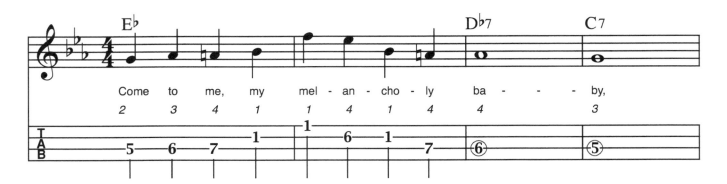

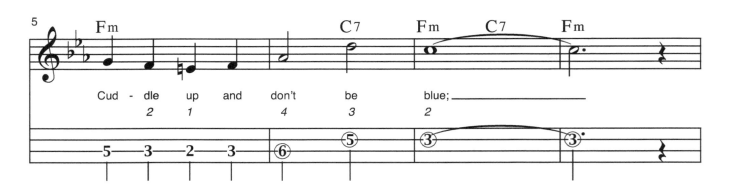

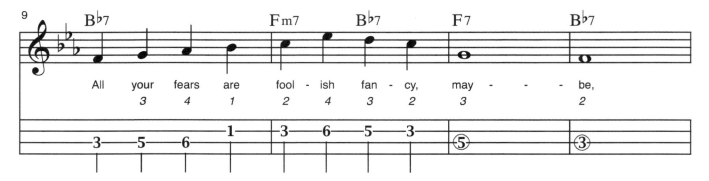

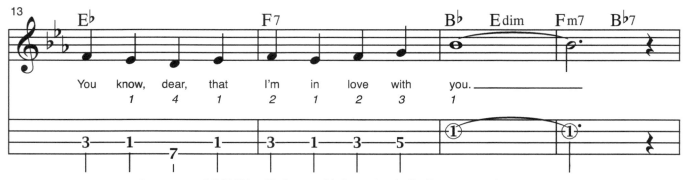

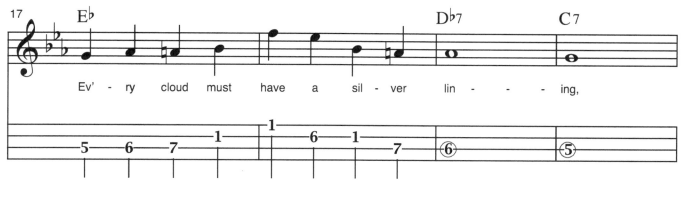

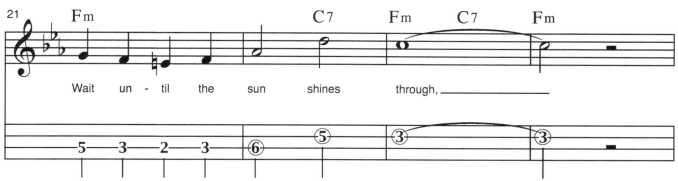

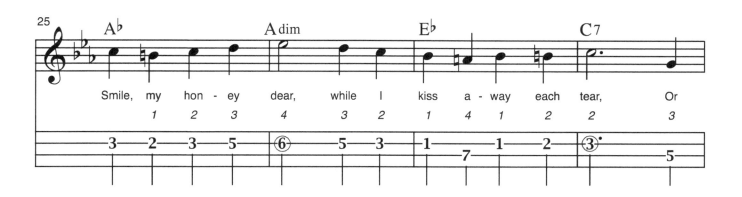

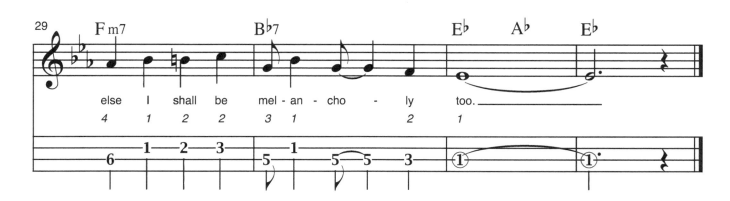

A Note on Improvising

As we progress as lead players most of us get to the point where we ask ourselves, especially after we've played the melody, "Now what do I play? How do I improvise?" I've mentioned different approaches throughout this book and think it might be worthwhile to list some of them again.

First of all, the melody is of the utmost importance. The melody *is* the song and what distinguishes it from every other song. Be sure to memorize each melody and don't be afraid to use it. The melody is always appropriate and always a good starting place for your improvisations.

I've mentioned "rhythmizing" melodies several times. "Rhythmizing" means to take a melody as written, keep the pitches pretty much the same, but change the rhythms. Maybe change a whole note to four quarters or vice versa. Repeat notes with different rhythmic patterns. Of course you can change the pitches of the notes too, but the idea is to keep as much of the original melody as possible. Once you have a solo that's rhythmized you can develop more solos that move further away from the melody or rhythmized melody. No matter how far you take your improvisations, it's best to develop your flights of fancy from a solid concept of the melody.

Work out an octave version of the melody by playing a melody note and simultaneously adding the same note an octave above or below it. Django, as well as just about every other modern guitar player, used this exciting technique to build exciting solos. Why not develop it on the mandolin? See page 49 for more on playing octaves.

Try turning the melody into a chord melody. You worked on some very limited chord melody passages in "Clouds and Shadows" (page 54) and "Stumbling" (page 81). With chord melody you place the melody note on strings one or two by choosing a chord where the melody note is the highest note of the chord.

Another boon to improvising is to know and understand the chord progression. Learn the notes of each chord and where they are located on the fingerboard in more than one position, if possible. Use the chord arpeggios to make up solos. Practice arpeggios ascending and descending beginning on every note of the arpeggio, not just the root. Make up patterns from these notes. Add in the neighboring tones from the associated scale between the chord tones. Remember: chord arpeggios will always work and never sound wrong when played over the corresponding chords. The trick is to make them sound melodic and not like an exercise.

Scales are also very important to learn. Practicing them teaches you where scale tones are located on the fingerboard. Start by learning basic major scales at as many positions as your instrument allows. Learn to play them in different positions starting with your first finger, then second finger, then third, and fourth playing the root. All the notes of some scales/positions may not be reachable without switching positions. Play them ascending and descending. Learn the three forms of the minor scale: natural, harmonic, and melodic the same way.

The most important advice I can give, which I've mentioned earlier, is to keep playing. Jam with the recorded band as often as you can — daily is best. Play rhythm chords, melodies, your own leads. Keep listening to all types of music. Find people to jam with. Try to find inspiration in what other players do and make it a part of your own musical vocabulary. And, most of all, find the fun in the music.

Way Down Yonder in New Orleans

"Way Down Yonder in New Orleans" is another big hit from the 1920s that became a multi-generational standard. Freddy "Boom Boom" Cannon made it into a teen dance hit in 1959. It's up to you to make it into a smasheroo in the 2020s!

The first part of the song starts, somewhat unusually, on a C7 chord, the dominant seven chord in the key of F. It's like "Avalon" on page 13 in that sense. On the first beat of measures thirteen and seventeen the band begins an eight beat, two measure rhythm break played on every chorus. Jason keeps a rhythmic click going to keep us in time.

My favorite part of the song is in measures twenty-one through twenty-four where the chord progression goes from F to Dm, the relative minor, then back to F and on to a very unexpected but very nice Db7.

On the up-to-speed version of the melody I rhythmize extensively and also add a few pickup notes at the beginning of the first phrase. "Way Down Yonder in New Orleans" is a good one to move up an octave.

We added an ending with the chords F – D7 – G7 – C7 – F to the band track. Musicians call this kind of ending by a variety of names. I've heard it called "around the horn," "one, six, two, five" (see note on numbering chords on page 42), and "cycle of fifths." It is a typical ending that you'll hear a lot on swing and jazz. Played by Band #2.

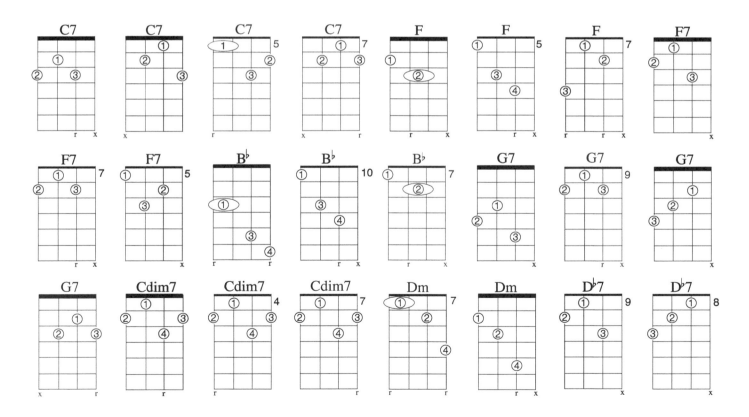

Way Down Yonder in New Orleans

Key of F

Creamer and Layton, 1922

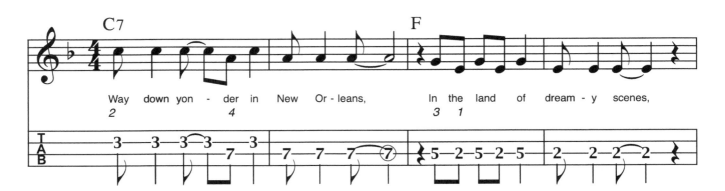

Way down yon - der in New Or - leans, In the land of dream - y scenes,

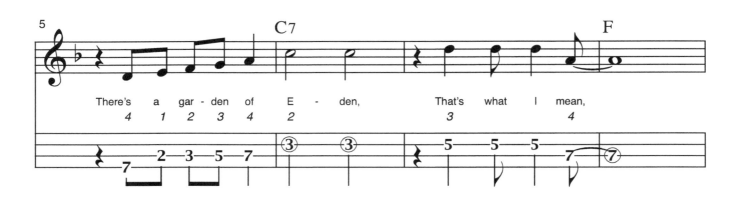

There's a gar - den of E - den, That's what I mean,

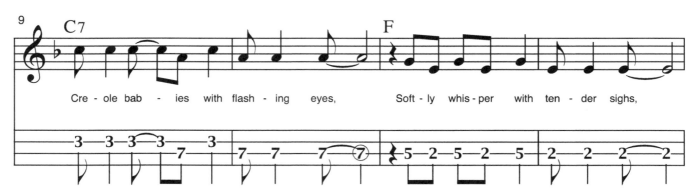

Cre - ole bab - ies with flash - ing eyes, Soft - ly whis - per with ten - der sighs,

Break on melody

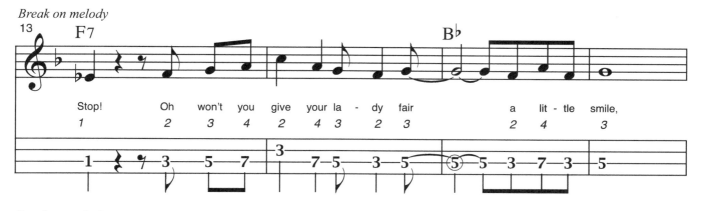

Stop! Oh won't you give your la - dy fair a lit - tle smile,

Break on melody

Stop! you bet your life you'll lin - ger there a lit - tle while.

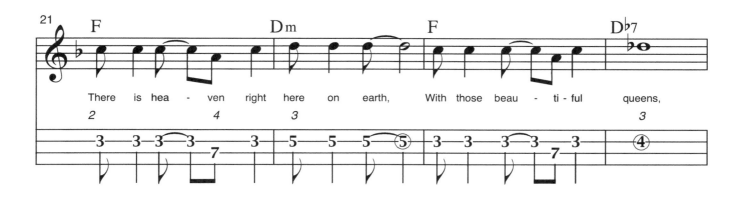

There is hea - ven right here on earth, With those beau - ti - ful queens,

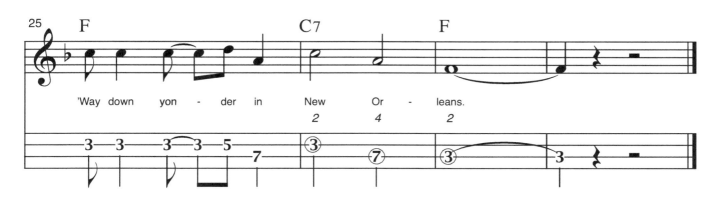

'Way down yon - der in New Or - leans.

The World is Waiting for the Sunrise

"The World is Waiting for the Sunrise" has long been a hot and fast show piece for instrumentalists, notably tenor banjo players. I remember seeing such a performance in Reno, NV, in the mid-1970s. The show was a pretty typical mix of recognizable older pop songs and fast-paced, slightly racy humor, played by a band clothed in late teens, early 1920s red and green plaids. The climax of the show featured the banjo player on this song. If memory serves, the band began the song at a moderate tempo. Suddenly the house lights went out, a red light inside the banjo got flipped on, backlighting the banjo player's strumming hand as the band doubled or tripled the tempo. Maximum entertainment was enjoyed by all!

On the recordings we play "The World is Waiting for the Sunrise" in cut time, just like in "Avalon" on page 13, among others in this book. I counted the slow version as "1 – 2 – 3 – 4 – 1 and 2 and 3 and 4 and" and the up-to-speed versions as "1 – 2 – 1 – 2 – 3 – 4." Once you learn the song you should experiment with different feels and tempos. "The World is Waiting for the Sunrise" works great as a ballad and lends itself well to a chord melody solo.

I especially like the G7 augmented chord in measures one and eight. The G7+ is here because the melody note it accompanies is a D#. D# is the augmented fifth note of the G7 chord and when you play it over a G7 chord you turn that chord into a G7+ or G7 augmented.

I also like the Cdim7 in measures two and ten. It's a little unusual and certainly unexpected, but little touches like these make a song interesting and memorable. Try all four different positions of the Cdim7. Only the first two are shown, but surround them with nearby versions of the other chords.

Augmented seventh and diminished seven chords can be a challenge to solo over. Just remember: with these chords (or with any other chords for that matter) the melody will always work. Chord tones will also always work and both will sound good.

The suggested fretting fingerings will give you a pinky workout. You could play most of these notes as open-string notes, but in doing so you'll sacrifice the ability to easily move the melody up and down the fingerboard.

Although I've been browbeating you about it throughout this entire book, I feel compelled to remind you one more time to move the melody up an octave. And down an octave. Can you move the melody and chord progression to different keys up and down or across the fingerboard? How about a chord melody version with the melody notes located on the second and first strings? That said, my work here is done! Played by Band #1.

As I write this in 2020 "The World is Waiting for the Sunrise" seems an appropriate song to end this book. It's hopeful and forward looking, a message we need more than ever in these times.

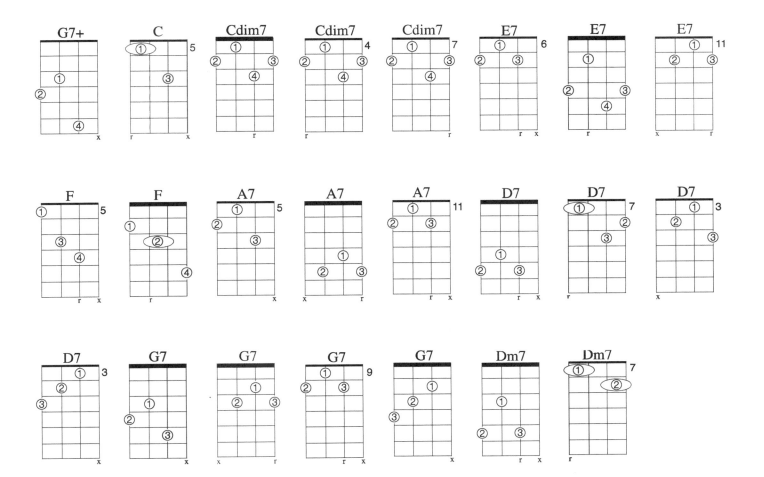

The World is Waiting for the Sunrise

Key of C

Seitz and Lockhart, 1919

Photo by Jim Nunally

Bob Schneider, left, with Dix Bruce, Portland, OR, 2006.
They're shown with two Schneider mandolins and a Schneider mandola.
Dix is holding the Schneider mandolin he played for "Gypsy Swing & Hot Club Rhythm."

Index

Django & Stephane's Recorded Solos & More

If you're interested in transcriptions of Django's recorded solos, see **The Music of Django Reinhardt: Forty Four Classic Solos by the Legandary Guitarist with Complete Analysis** (Mel Bay Publications) by Stan Ayeroff. (**musixnow.com/music-of-django-reinhardt-the**) It includes transcriptions of Django solos on most of the tunes in this book.

For transcriptions with guitar tablature of Django's original compositions, see **Complete Django: The Ultimate Django Book** (Bookmakers International) by Max Robin and Jean-Phillipe Watremez.

Violinists will enjoy 2 book/audio sets that Jeremy Cohen and I wrote based on **Gypsy Swing and Hot Club Rhythm** titled **Swing Jazz Violin with Hot Club Rhythm** (**musixnow.com/swing-jazz-violin-with-hot-club-rhythm-2**) and **Make Your Fiddle Swing: Solos and Duets for Violin,** (**musixnow.com/make-your-fiddle-swing**). They include songs from the two volumes of this book arranged for violin, plus additional titles, solos, and jazz string quartet arrangements.

Many of Stephane Grappelli's recorded solos are transcribed in Matt Glazer's book **Jazz Violin** (Oak Publications).

Gypsy Swing and Hot Club Rhythm Complete Guitar Edition

Gypsy Swing and Hot Club Rhythm Complete is also available in a version for guitarists. Same great songs with guitar tablature and commentary specially aimed at our six-string buddies. (musixnow.com/gypsy-swing-hot-club-rhythm-complete-guitar-edition/)

Made in United States
Troutdale, OR
11/16/2023

14619429R00064